YOU'VE HEARD HER VOICE

#1 in sales

BLUE

"There's certainly nothing immature about Rimes's voice. Range, tone, power, timing, soul: she's got it all."
—*Houston Chronicle*

#1 on radio

"ONE WAY TICKET (BECAUSE I CAN)"

"Rimes's performance . . . elevates the song from other female, uptempo country radio fare. The impressive set of pipes she displays on her ballads serves her well on this tune."
—*Billboard*

LeAnn's latest #1 hit

"UNCHAINED MELODY"
A classic she makes new again.

NOW READ THE INCREDIBLE STORY!

By Jo Sgammato
Published by Ballantine Books:

DREAM COME TRUE: The LeAnn Rimes Story
KEEPIN' IT COUNTRY: The George Strait Story
COUNTRY'S GREATEST DUO: The Brooks & Dunn Story

DREAM
COME
TRUE

The LeAnn Rimes Story

Jo Sgammato

BALLANTINE BOOKS • NEW YORK

To my music man,
Ira Fraitag.
For helping to make my dream come true.

—*J.S.*

http://www.randomhouse.com

Library of Congress Catalog Card Number: 97-93060

ISBN 9780345472762

Manufactured in the United States of America

Cover photo © John Chiasson/People Weekly

146673257

Acknowledgments

My wonderful editor, Cathy Repetti, and I have been publishing colleagues for longer than either of us would wish to say. It is a pleasure to work with her again.

The professionals at Ballantine Books, where I spent the happiest years of my own publishing career, are the best in the business. It is an honor to have my book in their hands.

I would also like to offer special thanks and sincere appreciation to:

• Ira Fraitag and Entertainment Management Group for guidance, music business background, and sharp ideas
• Lori Dean and the Exceptional Children Project for pursuing valuable work and providing invaluable research
• The Mississippi Department of Archives and History in

Jackson and libraries everywhere for keeping our heritage alive and accessible
- Marcus Bowers, editor of the *Rankin County* (Mississippi) News, for great leads
- Judith Mandelbaum, Vice-President, Research Services, Burrelle's Information Services, for her work, advice, and patience
- *Definitive Country: The Ultimate Encyclopedia of Country Music and Its Performers*, Barry McCloud and contributing writers, Bumper Books USA/Perigee Books, 1995, for everything its title delivers
- My husband, parents, sister, siblings-in-law, niece, nephews, great big family, and dear friends for, as LeAnn wrote in one of her songs, "more love than anyone deserves"

And a special wish for my godson, Alex: May you have big dreams, too.

Author's Note

I heard the "buzz" in Nashville about an incredible young singer that Curb Records had signed. Being in Nashville for the past several years with my husband, an artists' manager and record producer, I've spent time in the city's restaurants and clubs and in offices on Music Row.

Like everyone else, my first reaction was, Who is this thirteen-year-old?

Then I heard "Blue" and got part of the answer.

That voice singing that song only made me more curious about the singer. Then Ballantine Books gave me the opportunity to go out and learn about LeAnn Rimes.

Seeing LeAnn Rimes at Fan Fair in Nashville in June 1996 and listening to the other songs she sang on the album *Blue* told me there was something special to write about here.

For many years, I had worked in the book publishing business. I loved being involved on a daily basis, bringing the creative work of authors—books—to the public. Living in Nashville with the chance to observe the music business firsthand, it occurred to me that bringing out records—the creative work of musical artists—wasn't all that different.

Asking the question of how a young singer became such a huge star would enable me to learn and write about the world of music. For someone who's been singing along—and living my life—to thousands of great songs beginning when I first snuck a transistor radio under my pillow way past bedtime, it sounded like too much fun.

I asked a lot of questions, spoke to a lot of people, read a lot, listened a lot, and thought a lot about LeAnn Rimes. I traveled to her real hometown of Pearl, Mississippi, and her adopted home in the metro area of Dallas, Texas.

Being fortunate enough to know so many music-business professionals, I asked them to explain some of the things I was curious about and thought other "civilians" might also want to know. Their generosity has helped me understand and write about what it takes to go from a great demo tape to a spin at the top of the world. If I've gotten any of it wrong, it's my fault and not theirs.

And if I started this book as a fan of LeAnn Rimes, I've finished it filled with awe, respect, admiration, and love for her. Her gigantic talent is only part of what makes her one of the most extraordinary human beings around—of any age.

LeAnn's parents, Wilbur and Belinda Rimes, must be extraordinary people. Their only child told them she wanted to sing and be a star. Then they put everything they had on the line and helped her make it happen. That LeAnn is a star today is surprising enough given how hard it is and how little they knew about the music business when they started. That she is such a polished and generous young woman says a lot about Wilbur and Belinda Rimes.

You can't spend this much time tracing the details of someone's life and writing about her every day for months and months without feeling close to her. Although we've never met, I'd like to say this to LeAnn:

Thank you for showing that dreams do come true.

Thank you for giving us so much beautiful music.

Thank you for being such a joy to write about.

And may this be only the beginning.

Contents

CHAPTER ONE
Nashville Saturday Night
1

CHAPTER TWO
Child of Mississippi
8

CHAPTER THREE
Dazzling Dallas
31

CHAPTER FOUR
Starbound
55

CHAPTER FIVE
"Blue" Is Red-Hot
75

CHAPTER SIX
Dream Come True
101

CHAPTER SEVEN
Because I Can
137

CHAPTER ONE

☆ ☆ ☆

Nashville Saturday Night

The lights dimmed inside the sparkling new Nashville Arena. The crowd began to cheer, anticipating another great night of music in Music City. All eyes were on the stage as the announcer's booming voice filled the hall.

"Ladies and gentlemen, put your hands together and give a great big Nashville welcome to Miss LeAnn Rimes!"

Preparation for the evening's show—for which twenty thousand fans would be packed inside the Arena—had begun at ten o'clock that morning when a line of forty-foot tractor trailers exited Interstate 40 at Demonbreun Street, drove downtown, and pulled into the loading dock of the Arena.

They were met by the local stage crew for the "load-in." Fifty or sixty trunks, each prominently displaying a white number, were rolled to the stage area. Trunks filled with the T-shirts and tour books fans love to collect went to the lobby. The crews—sound, lights, and merchandising—started getting ready for the show.

* * *

The Nashville Arena on Broadway is the latest addition to the shimmering multimillion-dollar restoration
of downtown Music City. It's up the street from Planet
Hollywood and the Hard Rock Cafe and within honking
distance of the Wildhorse Saloon. Country line-dancing
shows on TNN broadcast the fun of the Wildhorse into
homes across America. Near the banks of the
Cumberland River, the area known in Nashville as the
District is turning into a flashy entertainment and residential area after years of neglect and decline.

In Nashville, there are dozens if not hundreds of ways
to spend a Saturday night. Almost every type of live
music is played in almost any kind of setting. If you're
an artist, you'll find Nashville a tough place to perform.
Some of the world's best players and singers call the city
and its surrounding counties home.

The headliner at the Arena on this Saturday night in
February was Alan Jackson, a down-home superstar and
winner of seven Country Music Association Awards,
including Entertainer of the Year and Album of the Year.
Alan Jackson's special guest, whose fans were plenty
excited themselves, was LeAnn Rimes—the biggest new
country star of the year of any age. And her age was fourteen.

By two o'clock in the afternoon, when the Arena
crews broke for lunch, the stage, the sound equipment,
and the lights were set up. The merchandise was
unpacked and on display. The tour accountant and tour

manager had checked the box office and met with the local concert promoter. Security personnel were assigned to their posts.

Alan Jackson and LeAnn Rimes had toured together very successfully in 1996 and were already booked for at least thirty-two Arena-size dates in '97. Alan Jackson has ruled the country charts since 1990 and boasts the biggest fan club in country music. LeAnn Rimes is the youngest performer in country-music history to debut at number one on the sales chart with her first major album. That album was *Blue*.

LeAnn and her band arrived for their sound check. Before every show a band does a sound check to make sure a clear sound can be heard throughout the audience. Working with all the instruments individually and then together, the sound engineers, like jewelers, created a perfect setting for the precious gem on display here tonight—LeAnn's voice.

Dressing rooms in arenas are all the same and not very glamorous. Singers might dress one night in the same place hockey players took their socks off the previous night. The road cases carrying LeAnn's stage wardrobe were opened and ready for her selection. LeAnn says she loves to shop. She told *Prime Time Country*'s Gary Chapman that she travels with a busload of clothes. Tight black jeans, a V-neck black knit top, and shiny black shoes were the ensemble she chose for tonight's performance.

In the hospitality room where LeAnn would make an appearance before the show, platters of catered food and various beverages were already set up. There were important people for LeAnn to greet at every show. But in Nashville, top staff from the record company, public-relations firm, and booking agency were key guests whenever an artist came to town. Maintaining the friendship, faith, and belief of the folks who handle your records and live appearances is essential—and fun.

MCG/Curb Records, Rogers & Cowan Public Relations, and Creative Artists Agency had a lot to celebrate with LeAnn Rimes.

Together they had just achieved one of the most phenomenal entertainment success stories of all time.

As LeAnn strode onto the stage and into the glow of the spotlight, the Arena exploded in whistles, hollers, screams, stomps, and applause. Seconds later, the crowd sat silently while she sang "Blue Moon of Kentucky" a cappella. When the band joined in on the third chorus, the tune turned rockabilly and the foot stomping started all over again.

LeAnn sang two more songs from her latest album release. Her warmth, presence, and soaring voice won every heart in the house, from the ten-year-olds waving illuminated red roses to the parents and grandparents who loved her like she was their own.

"Thank you. Thank you very much," she said, bowing with perfect grace. Her wireless microphone held lightly between her fingers as she raised it to her lips, she lifted her eyes toward heaven during "Hurt Me," a ballad from *Blue*. Throughout the set, she introduced the members of her band graciously and generously, saying something special about each one.

When she broke into her hit single "One Way Ticket (Because I Can)," all those who'd heard its triumphant lyric on the radio became her backup singers. She walked the stage, making a stop to groove with each musician. Then she finished with a flourish by hitting the cymbals with her hands.

Two classics, the Ben E. King hit "Stand by Me" and the Hank Williams signature song, "I'm So Lonesome I Could Cry," became, in LeAnn's renditions, touchstones for new fans.

"I love you, Nashville," she shouted from the stage. "Thanks to all of you for calling and requesting my first single. And thanks to country radio for playing 'Blue.'"

The song "Blue" was originally written for country legend Patsy Cline, who died before she could record it. Thirty years later, LeAnn Rimes's version of the song turned the country-music business on its ear.

Now LeAnn sang her history-making version of that old song on a Saturday night in Music City's hottest new venue. Just as she'd done all evening, she commanded the stage with the poise, presence, and delivery of someone who'd been there all her life.

LeAnn Rimes became the number one Country Singles Sales Artist of the Year with "Blue." She accomplished more in one year—no, make that ten months— than most performers achieve in a lifetime.

Her album of the same name debuted at number one on the *Billboard* country charts and spent an amazing nineteen weeks there, more than any other album during the year. Though the country-music business closed out

1996 with a twelve-percent drop in sales, LeAnn Rimes was selling records faster than her company could press them.

She was the youngest artist ever nominated for a Country Music Association Award. She was the *only* country artist with a Grammy nomination for Best New Artist of the Year. And, when the envelope was opened, she had won. In *Rolling Stone*'s Readers Poll for Best Country Artist of the Year, she came in second—behind Johnny Cash.

LeAnn's first major-label album sold as many copies as albums by such pop stars as Metallica and Celine Dion. It went gold in England, double platinum in Canada, and triple platinum in Australia, where she was proclaimed that country's best-selling female country-music artist of all time.

The Early Years, her new early 1997 release, containing a mixture of old and new cuts, enjoyed a first-week sales performance matched only by Garth Brooks and the Beatles.

The first country-music star born in the 1980s, LeAnn Rimes was called a "teenage singing sensation" everywhere she went in 1996.

But there's much more to LeAnn Rimes than that. If she performs like a pro, it's because she hasn't spent more than two or three weekends without being on a stage since she was six years old. If she sings with the most incredible voice anyone has heard in years, it's because God blessed her with a miraculous instrument and a rare gift that she learned how to use, virtually all by herself. If she's made it to the top and beyond in such a short time, it's because she and her parents have been working toward this moment ever since she declared at the age of five that she was going to sing and become a big star.

LeAnn asked the audience to listen carefully to a song she'd just written because the lyrics meant so much to her. "I've been loved more than anyone deserves," she sang.

"I remember watching Reba and all the big stars, thinking hopefully I'll be up there someday," LeAnn has said.

This is the story of how LeAnn Rimes, with a lot of help from her family, her fans, and God, made her dream come true.

CHAPTER TWO

☆ ☆ ☆

Child of Mississippi

About twelve years before and a seven-hour drive from the Nashville Arena, LeAnn Rimes had a different audience. Much smaller than the crowd of twenty thousand who watched her in Nashville, it nevertheless contained enough love to fill twenty Arenas.

In the living room of the home of her grandparents, Thad and Annie Jewel Butler, the beautiful blond eighteen-month-old sat in her baby seat and belted out a song, "Jesus Loves Me." Wilbur Rimes and the former Belinda Butler, LeAnn's parents, as well as other relatives and friends, could only watch and listen in amazement.

Like all kids who love music, LeAnn also sang in the car.

"It's something every mother would probably love to see her little girl do," Belinda Rimes said. "I've seen her when she was a little girl wake up in the backseat, get up and sing, and lie right back down and go to sleep." One of LeAnn's favorite songs to sing in the car was "Just a Swingin'."

Wilbur Rimes has tapes of LeAnn singing accompanied by his guitar before she was two years old. "She just came here singing," he said. "Early on, I knew that gal had a gift."

Wilbur doesn't just play guitar. He sings, and it's been said that he has perfect pitch. He says the only place he sings these days is in the shower.

When she listens to the tapes from her very early years, LeAnn finds them "kind of cute. I could sing better than I could talk. You could understand every word when I was singing. But you couldn't understand what I was saying when I talked."

As a little girl born after the invention of the compact disc, LeAnn used to go to her grandmother's and listen to records. Her early favorites were country singers Reba McEntire, Wynonna, and Patsy Cline. But even then, LeAnn's tastes ventured beyond country. She loved listening to Barbra Streisand and Judy Garland.

In January 1997, in the same living room where LeAnn used to sing, Thad Butler related the story of LeAnn's early years with a beaming smile on his face, every inch the proud grandfather. LeAnn calls him PawPaw.

Thad Butler is a tall, strong man. He moved to the Mississippi town he calls home when he was seventeen and has been there ever since. He was warm in his invitation to "come in" and "sit down" on that Sunday morning. He'd been out in the driveway looking under the hood of his car, whose back fender sports a LeAnn Rimes bumper sticker.

Thad Butler runs his own business out on Highway 80. Butler's Portable Buildings sells outdoor storage units of all sizes. It's just a few doors down from George's Family Restaurant. Mr. Butler is well known to the people at the chamber of commerce and to many other folks in town. He's a member of the First Baptist Church.

The town proud to have given the world LeAnn Rimes is Pearl, Mississippi. Just a few minutes east of Jackson, the state capital, Pearl is a small Southern town with memories of a slower, simpler past and a current spurt of growth and development similar to that experienced by communities all over America. Pearl covers many square miles but has no real town square or center. Many new businesses have come to Pearl over the last four years—Thad Butler attributes that growth to "low interest rates"—and are crowded onto Highway 80 and on Pearson Road, which connects Highway 80 with Interstate Route 20. Incorporated in 1973, Pearl's town slogan is "Unity, Prosperity, Progress."

Belinda Rimes and her sister, Melissa, grew up in Thad and Annie Jewel Butler's house in the 1950s and 1960s, when Pearl was still small. The house is a lovely example of the sort found all over Pearl. Built of brick on neat, well-cared-for yards, the houses are mostly one story—it was too hot before the days of air-conditioning to have an upstairs.

The atmosphere inside the Butler family home is warm and cozy. Lovely silk flower arrangements surround the overstuffed living-room furniture. Family pictures grace the tabletops and dot the walls.

What appears to be a high school picture of Belinda Butler Rimes shows a smiling and beautiful young woman with blond hair, blue eyes, and luminous skin. In another picture, Belinda and Wilbur are together, looking very much in love and, like so many young couples, hopeful for the future. As a young man perhaps just entering his twenties, Wilbur C. Rimes looks like someone who works hard, believes in God, and is committed to doing the best he can for his new young wife.

There's a picture of Wilbur looking proud in his cream-colored Stetson and Belinda looking sharp in a great red sweater and a black blouse with a big bow tie under her neck. But the real scene-stealer here (and no doubt the Rimeses would agree!) is five-month-old LeAnn, who displays all the joy and enthusiasm for life that would soon propel her into an amazing career.

Hanging on the wall above the television, where Thad Butler can watch his granddaughter's music videos several times a day, are even more pictures of LeAnn Rimes as a baby and child.

On this Sunday morning, Thad Butler's house is filled with the mouthwatering smell of potatoes baking in the kitchen. Dark wooden cabinets, gleaming appliances, and a round wooden table surrounded by chairs make the kitchen look as homey as it smells.

"She could really sing," Thad says. "It's a God-given talent. She said she was someday going to take it and sing around the world."

LeAnn was blessed with confidence. Someone upstairs must have known she would need it where she was going in life. She wasn't the least bit shy and was always ready to sing for anyone who'd listen. "She never met a stranger," her granddaddy says.

The smiling face of Thad Butler reveals instantly that he's a close relation to LeAnn Rimes. Both have the same tilt to their head. Each has the crinkly eyes of people who really mean it when they smile. You can always fake a smile with your mouth, but it's from those smiling eyes that a real one radiates. Told that LeAnn is the spitting image of her PawPaw, Mr. Butler smiles even wider.

Belinda Butler and Wilbur Rimes were high school sweethearts who attended McLauren High School, at the edge of Pearl where Highway 80 enters Brandon, the next town. In the late 1960s, Pearl and Brandon were still very small towns, but they did have their own weekly newspaper, which also covered news in the nearby towns of Flowood and Pelahatchie. The slogan of the *Rankin County News* back then was "The Only Newspaper in the World Interested in the Progress of Rankin County."

In addition to reporting on town and county government, business news, and local sports, the paper carried announcements of engagements and weddings, club meetings, and other community activities. Long columns detailed who had visited whom over the past week, even visits to the next town to the homes of relatives for a few hours on Saturday afternoon.

The paper offered extensive coverage of the local schools and in the spring of 1969 included the name Belinda Butler in its list of the junior class honor roll. It also covered the numerous beauty pageants and talent contests that take place in small towns and big cities all over the United States but that seem to be an even stronger thread in the fabric of life in the South.

In 1970, the year she graduated from high school, Belinda Butler married Wilbur Rimes. She went to work as a receptionist. He had a job selling equipment for an oil company.

They settled in Pearl and their lives took on the usual routines of working, visiting with friends and relatives, and attending the First Baptist Church on Sundays. Then as now, religion was a big part of life in every community in the South, which seems to have more churches of more denominations than anywhere else. After church, families all over Rankin County sit down to a midday Sunday dinner, where, after saying grace, they enjoy the great home cooking for which the South is famous.

Wilbur owned coon dogs and enjoyed going hunting with his buddies. He also loved listening to music and playing the guitar. Did he ever have dreams of being a star?

For the first ten years of their marriage, Wilbur and Belinda tried to have a child, unfortunately without success. Belinda saw all the married women her age having children and wondered, "Why not me?"

Belinda began praying for a child in the twelfth year of her marriage. "Six and a half weeks later, I found out I was pregnant."

LeAnn Rimes was born on August 28, 1982, at Rankin County Hospital on Highway 80, about seven miles from Pearl. "She was a miracle in more ways than one," Belinda says.

Adds Wilbur, "She was worth the wait."

LeAnn's official first name is Margaret, in honor of her godmother, Margaret Ray, according to Thad Butler. Margaret's husband, Gerald Ray, is LeAnn's godfather.

In her first year of life, LeAnn enjoyed the adoration of all the Butlers and Rimeses and other members of their extended families. Sitting on her MawMaw's lap at the age of one, LeAnn waved and smiled at the camera. The pictures in her granddaddy's home show a bright-eyed, happy, smiling child. "When she came along, we just devoted our whole life to her," Belinda said.

Then, at eighteen months, LeAnn started to sing. And during her preschool years she sang every day, according to her granddaddy, at home, in church, and in shows all over Rankin County.

"I knew she was going to be a star," Thad Butler says today. "I didn't know it would happen this fast."

Maybe it was because Wilbur was always playing records at home. Belinda was always singing to LeAnn, too. Maybe those moments captured LeAnn's young imagination. Or maybe, as so many people have said, LeAnn Rimes was simply born to sing.

The fertile ground of Mississippi has given us many musical artists whose impact on popular music has been great. W. C. Handy, Muddy Waters, and Robert Johnson, three of the greatest bluesmen, all hail from Clarksdale, near the legendary Highway 61, in northwest Mississippi. Another young man, born in Tupelo in the state's northeast corner, changed not only music but the entire world. His name was Elvis Presley.

LeAnn Rimes is the artistic descendant of these and other musical giants born under the sunny blue umbrella of the Mississippi sky.

MISSISSIPPI MUSICIANS
WHO MADE HISTORY

JIMMY BUFFETT
Born in Pascagoula

JOHNNY CARVER
Near Jackson

MICKEY GILLEY
Natchez

FAITH HILL
Jackson

CHRIS LEDOUX
Biloxi

CHARLIE PRIDE
Sledge

JIMMIE RODGERS
Near Meridian

MARTY STUART
Philadelphia

CONWAY TWITTY
Friars Point

BOBBIE GENTRY
Chickasaw County

BOBBIE GENTRY

Of all her creative comrades from Mississippi, LeAnn started out having more in common with Bobbie Gentry than with the others. And later in her life, LeAnn would have her name linked with Bobbie's for more than just coming from the same state.

Bobbie Gentry is a beautiful woman of Portuguese descent. Her given name was Roberta Streeter. Her talent—and one song—propelled her onto the international stage in 1967 with an astonishing debut single.

"Ode to Billy Joe" was a song that had so many elements, so many dimensions that it became one of the most talked about and scrutinized popular hits of all time.

Gentry wrote it herself.

Raised in a farmhouse in Chickasaw County by her grandparents, Bobbie had a talent that was obvious by the time she was seven years old. Farm life was hard and her grandfolks were poor. But they saw something special.

So they traded a cow for a piano, and Bobbie taught herself to play by watching the local church pianist. She wrote her first song that year: "My Dog Sergeant Is a Good Dog."

When Bobbie was thirteen, the family moved to Palm Springs, California, where she acquired more instrumental skills and started performing in local clubs. She attended UCLA and majored in philosophy, playing the occasional gig to pay for her studies.

After seeing the movie *Ruby Gentry*, Bobbie took on her performing name. That year, Capitol signed her, and her first single was "Ode to Billy Joe."

We can talk all day about the meaning of the song and it wouldn't be the first time that happened. Although events on the Tallahatchie Bridge have never been clarified, we do know the song became a huge hit in 1967.

And Bobbie Gentry became the first country female to score a number one album on the *Billboard* 200 Chart.

LeAnn began to direct her climb to success even before she entered school. Her parents say she's the one who pushed them, not vice versa.

At the age of two, LeAnn began taking tap-dance lessons. Beverly's School of Dance and Baton has studios in Pearl and in Brandon. The Pearl studio is on Highway 80, just across the road from Butler's Portable Buildings.

The studios are similar: lots of pretty pink paint, an outer reception area, a dressing room, and the actual practice studio with ballet barres of two different heights to accommodate students of all ages and sizes. Each studio displays many certificates, citations, awards, and trophies. Beverly Smith, the owner and chief instructor, is a vivacious blonde with a great dancer's body that makes her look younger than her years.

On a Monday night in January 1997, the Brandon studio was bustling. Beverly was teaching some adorable young girls in the studio a series of steps set to soul-music tunes. More were waiting for their classes to begin. They were all dressed in leotards and tights and each had some kind of jazzy headband or clip or barrette in her hair. Proud mamas were nearby chatting about their daughters and their progress.

Before joining her five-thirty class, Beverly recalled when LeAnn had studied dance at her studio. She was sitting behind her counter in the outer reception room, which is decorated with wallpaper showing girls in different ballet poses. A wonderful framed needlepoint of ballet slippers included the words *To dance is to dream.*

Beverly smiled at her memories of LeAnn. "She was just like she is now, sweet-natured, and a good child."

When LeAnn first started taking lessons, was it clear she'd someday be a star?

"You don't know," Beverly said. "When they start at three, I look in the class and think, 'Who will stay with me or who will do what?' and sometimes it's not the best ones who will stay with you, pursuing the dance and the talent shows. You just don't know. Some of them that you think are wonderful at three, by the time they get to be six, they've gone on to something else."

When she was four, LeAnn tap-danced in a show, wearing a red gingham dress and a big red gingham bow in her hair. Her hair was so blond and sparkling it looked almost white. Her face, so confident and beautiful, takes your breath away, even today.

Beverly Smith encouraged Belinda and Wilbur to take LeAnn's talents out into the world of competitions. LeAnn always asked her mama and daddy to dress her up in frilly dresses and let her perform.

"LeAnn wanted to perform every place she could," her godmother, Margaret Ray, said.

According to Belinda, "It was like LeAnn knew what she came into this world wanting to do."

Kids are always saying what they want to be when they grow up. Sometimes these ideas are not more than passing fancies. Often they are pure fantasy. Sometimes they are simply too dangerous or downright impossible. Some children's dreams are too far out of the financial reach of their parents ever to realize.

In the case of children with artistic talents, money alone is no guarantee of success. The road they're taking is a road that has been traveled many times before, a dark, lonely ribbon of concrete littered with disappointment, financial hardship, and broken hearts. How do parents know which dreams to take seriously and which ones to discourage? If they decide to help further a child's dream, how do parents like Wilbur and Belinda, with only a little musical knowledge and no real experience in show business, go about it?

Wilbur's love of music played a big part in his recognition of LeAnn's great potential. Some parents wouldn't be able to distinguish true talent from simple pride in the sight of a beautiful child singing. Wilbur was aware of many successful musicians and understood that you really could make a living as a singer and performer.

"The Rimeses made all the sacrifices they had to make for her," said Beverly Smith, who knew Wilbur and Belinda through LeAnn. "And I don't know how they knew how to pursue it. I think [that] they had so much confidence in her, and her voice is just phenomenal."

What does it take for any talented kid to make it? "Desire on the part of the child," Beverly said emphatically. "And encouragement from the parents. And I have a lot of parents who say, 'I'm not going to make her do it.' But I thank my mother every day that she made me do it.

"I'll tell you what, I've never seen a child be something without the mother or parents—I hate to say making them do it—encouraging them and supporting them. I know you can't make somebody do something they really don't want to do, but if they want to, you can reward them and encourage them to go ahead and do it."

LeAnn had started out dancing and singing. Though she could tap-dance very well, Thad Butler said, she concentrated more on singing.

"LeAnn did several of those shows where she sang and danced," he said. And if PawPaw and MawMaw were in the audience, they were sure to be cheering her on.

According to Ginny Kendrick of the Pearl Chamber

of Commerce, local businesses sponsored many of the contests in the area that offered a title and a trophy. The Pearl City Hall gym held frequent contests. The beauty and talent competitions would accept children as young as a few months old and as old as twenty-one. The judges were pageant professionals from the local area or, if the contest was big enough, from other parts of the country.

Talent shows, beauty pageants, and competitions for all kinds of titles and awards keep the three trophy shops in Pearl busy. Little Miss Pearl might seem like a small, local contest, featuring girls as young as three, but the winner could go on to become Little Miss Mississippi (if she beats Little Miss Brandon) or even Little Miss America. Some years, the Little Miss Mississippi Beauty and Talent Showcase sends some lucky winners to New York to audition for Broadway shows. Among the many contests the *Rankin County News* and the *Pearl Weekly Leader* report on—and often feature as front-page news—are Miss Summer Festival Queen, Miss Hospitality, and Miss Southern Majorette. There's even a Farm Bureau Talent contest and a contest that elects the Mississippi Pork Queen.

What was LeAnn like during these competitions? "She was confident onstage and performed just like a little professional," Beverly Smith said. "She was good to the other little children behind the stage, too.

"Being in pageants in the early years—I think being in pageants on the whole—helps children so much with their confidence level if it's handled correctly. Again it goes back to the parents. I think she was very talented and lucky, too. I think it takes a lot of both, and support from her parents. All the people in Pearl were very supportive, too."

It certainly made a difference in LeAnn's life that Pearl, unlike many small towns, was just a few miles from the state capital of Jackson. Jackson is a beautiful old Southern city with huge brick and stone houses and public buildings beautifully built in Greek Revival style.

Each month at least two major cultural events draw people into the city from Pearl, Brandon, and Flowood.

The Metropolitan Chamber Orchestra Society, the Mississippi Opera Association, and the Mississippi Symphony Orchestra reveal Jackson to be a sophisticated city. Jackson also boasts a Puppet Arts Theater, the Repertory Theater of Mississippi, the New Stage Theater, and Ballet Magnificat. Outdoor enthusiasts can play a variety of sports or visit the Planetarium and Space Theater or the Jackson Zoological Park.

From October 7 through 18, 1987, when LeAnn was five years old, the annual Mississippi State Fair took place at the Mississippi Coliseum and Fairgrounds, the oldest fairgrounds in the Southeast, located on Mississippi Street close to the edge of Flowood, the town just west of Pearl.

Although LeAnn was unable to enter the talent show, which was limited to ages nine to twenty-one, the talent that came to entertain Jackson was amazing enough to excite a young girl's imagination.

Country-music legends such as Conway Twitty, the Bellamy Brothers, and Sawyer Brown played the fair. The band Alabama showed Mississippi why they are one of the region's most beloved groups. Loretta Lynn and Tammy Wynette, two of the reigning queens of country music, sang with the passion that had made their own dreams come true.

Running parallel to Highway 80, Old Brandon Road used to be the main route between Pearl and Brandon. At the corner of Mary Ann Drive and Old Brandon Road is the City Park. Its wooden tables and benches, swings, and lovely grassy areas suggest a picnic on a quiet afternoon.

Down the road from the park and around the corner from LeAnn's grandparents' house is the Pearl Lower Elementary School. The school, like so many others built in the 1950s, is a low, flat red-brick building with lots of windows. A couple of ball fields are nearby. Farther down Mary Ann Drive is Pearl Junior High School.

Inside the main entrance of Pearl Lower Elementary School, walls are filled with students' artwork. Many little water fountains and long rows of classrooms look just like they did when LeAnn was a student here. The principal, John Morris, has been in charge of the school since before LeAnn entered kindergarten.

In the administration office, on a brisk winter Monday, a group of well-behaved youngsters was quietly waiting to buy some school supplies. Asked if they knew that a famous singing star had gone to this very school, they shook their heads as their eyes widened with interest.

"Do you know LeAnn Rimes?" No, these few didn't, but no doubt one day they will. And they'll surely be thrilled when they make the connection between LeAnn and one of their teachers—LeAnn's aunt Melissa. Now they know her as Mrs. Bagwell. Guess they don't know the significance of the LeAnn Rimes bumper sticker on her pickup truck.

The adults in the office do remember LeAnn, with smiles and twinkles in their eyes. She had sung in a program in the first grade and had been a good student.

After completing kindergarten, LeAnn's summer activities included an annual event that brought the whole town together in City Park. Pearl Day was held on Saturday, June 25, 1988.

Throughout the week before, there was a tennis tourney, and the finals were held on Saturday afternoon. The softball finals were on Saturday night. But the festivities really began on Friday night with the preopening ceremonies and a performance by the Parchman Band in City Park, just down the road from the Pearl Elementary School and around the corner from PawPaw's house.

On Saturday, the event that would most interest and excite the children began just after eight A.M. As it had done the year before, the Pearl Police Department sponsored a Kiddieland, with games and activities for the youngsters to enjoy in the park. Lieutenant Tobe Ivy and his fellow juvenile officer Dory May coordinated the event, according to the *Weekly Leader.* All the kids in LeAnn's kindergarten who went to Pearl Day must have loved the rides and games, the dart throw, the duck pond, the Ferris wheel, and the moonwalk.

"We're putting real low prices on those so the kids will be able to stretch their money and do more things," Lieutenant Ivy told the *Weekly Leader.* Face painting, a radar-timed baseball throw, and a bean toss sponsored by

Pizza Hut accompanied appearances by Smokey the Bear, McGruff the Crime Dog, the McDonald's Hamburglar, and even an Army National Guard helicopter on display. A children's barnyard, including piglets, a calf, a deodorized skunk, and other small animals, was manned by the Pelahatchie FFA Club. For a town so small, Pearl residents sure know how to put on a show. For LeAnn Rimes, who sang at the festival, it was one more example of the power of entertainment to bring miles of smiles to many faces.

For the rest of that summer, LeAnn pursued more singing and more talent shows.

At fourteen years old, Amy Arender Hogue had been teaching modeling and voice for two years. Her specialty was helping children prepare for competitions, pageants, and talent shows.

"Someone commissioned me to work with their child after a competition. Other people heard about me and I had a few students in LeAnn's area," she said.

"Parents would set up either a thirty- or sixty-minute session each week. We worked in studios where I rented space or sometimes we worked in my home."

Amy was delighted when she got the opportunity to work with LeAnn Rimes. At six, LeAnn was already well known locally for all the contests she'd won.

"We worked on two songs in particular," Amy explained. "'Somewhere Over the Rainbow' and 'Nickelodeon.' We worked on her breath control, on choreography, and on costuming."

In one local competition, she reported, "LeAnn sang the first part of 'Nickelodeon' and then tap-danced the rest."

Amy continued working privately with talented students in Rankin County. She studied in New York when she was seventeen and opened her own school, Mississippi Arts in Motion, three years ago at the age of nineteen.

"The idea of teaching was something I just couldn't get away from," she explained recently. "For me, the school is a dream come true."

Wilbur and Belinda began coming to terms with their beloved and long-awaited child having a dream in her heart too powerful to be denied.

"She was strong-willed and she was this-away—straight ahead, focused," Belinda said. "When you've got a child like that and you're not like that yourself, it kind of makes you that way. When you've been laid-back and easygoing, you've gotta roll with the flow and see what happens."

In the fall of 1988, LeAnn was back in Pearl Lower Elementary School as a first-grader. The *Weekly Leader,* in its December 7, 1988, issue, published a list of the students who'd made the honor roll. There, among the first graders who'd achieved all A's, was the name LeAnn Rimes.

Some six-year-olds recognize what can be attained with work and effort. For a child with a dream as big as LeAnn's, making the first-grade honor roll would only encourage the belief and strengthen the conviction that her dream could really come true.

"All little kids have dreams of what they want to do when they grow up," LeAnn says. "Mine never changed."

The *Weekly Leader* of Wednesday, December 21, 1988, published letters to Santa written by the students of Pearl Lower Elementary School. LeAnn told Santa that her family and her class loved him. She asked for some toys and some pets and closed with, "Please bring me all of the things that I want."

"She touched hearts everywhere she went," Belinda said. "People just fell in love with her."

Throughout first grade, LeAnn continued to perform in pageants and talent contests in Rankin and nearby Hinds counties. Wilbur has closets full of trophies and awards that LeAnn has won over the years. Winning may not be everything, but try telling that to a six-year-old who sees every triumph as another step on the road to realizing her dream.

LeAnn stood tall and proud as she posed for pictures draped in a banner, wearing a tiara, and carrying a bouquet of flowers and a trophy. Chalk another win up for our girl. She looked like a model with the perfect posture and poise others take years to attain.

To drive from Pearl to Flowood, you head west first on Highway 80, then on Route 468, a two-lane winding road. Many large factory buildings are headquarters to such businesses as industrial suppliers, the Stone Container Corporation, and some of the many steel mills in the Jackson area.

Wilbur drove down Route 468 with Belinda next to him. While her parents were always nervous for her, LeAnn had all the confidence of the seasoned contestant she had become. Dressed up, hair beautifully combed, LeAnn sat in the backseat reviewing her song and preparing for her performance as Wilbur made the final turn into the city of Flowood.

Talent contests were as big in Flowood as they were in Brandon. The Flowood Academy held many competitions at the Flowood Town Recreation Hall. Where there was a talent show, you could usually find the Rimeses.

Although she was up against children twice her age, LeAnn wasn't as dismayed as her parents about the seemingly stiff competition. With Wilbur and Belinda watching, she sang "Getting to Know You" from *The King and I.* Wilbur thought "she did okay," and left to go hunting for raccoons while LeAnn and Belinda waited for the judges to select the winner.

Later that day, Wilbur got home before his family. Soon after his return, the door opened and a six-foot-tall first-prize trophy was pushed inside by four-foot-tall LeAnn. Wilbur became quite emotional.

"Come on over here and talk to me, LeAnn," he said. "Is this really what you want to do?"

"Oh, yes, Daddy, it's all I ever want," LeAnn said. "I'm going to be a singer. I'm going to be a big star one day."

LeAnn was fortunate that Wilbur was such a music fan and a musician as well. He could relate to his daughter's love of music and her desire to sing. Some parents might not be able to see it like Wilbur could.

When she was five, LeAnn won a preliminary round of the Hemisphere Pageant in Rankin County. The state competition in Jackson took place at the Holiday Inn. Beverly Smith was a codirector.

"She was just darling then, the same as now. I think she was born singing; she's a natural. Her mother and daddy really had high hopes for her and her daddy was going to be her manager."

After LeAnn won overall talent in the state Hemisphere Pageant, Beverly Smith wanted her to go to the nationals in Florida. "I think they could win a car there," she said, "and we tried to put her in because that would be a good advertisement for us, to have a national winner. But her daddy said, 'No, we're taking her to Texas to make a star out of her.'"

What did Beverly Smith think about that idea? "Well, when her daddy said that, we just kind of said okay and didn't really think anything about it."

Amy Hogue said, "Way back then I knew the parents wanted it for her. They were willing to give everything up to help her."

Making the decision to move to Texas meant Belinda and Wilbur and their only child would be leaving their hometown, their families, their jobs, and everything familiar to them. They chose Dallas because its opries, rodeos, pageants, and honky-tonks had already launched many big showbiz careers.

What did Thad Butler think when his son-in-law told him he was taking his family to Texas to put little LeAnn on some bigger stages? Thad Butler indicated he'd had few objections. Add one more supporter to the team that had to be unanimous in the belief that stardom was within reach.

Parents are always willing to help their children, especially if, like Wilbur and Belinda, they've witnessed other children growing up to make it big in the music business. Read biographical portraits of almost any star, from musicians to sports heroes to great actors, and they all appear to have one thing in common: the unequivocal support of at least one parent. A child perhaps cannot sustain a big dream if the most influential people in her young life are expressing doubts and fears.

Belinda often tells people that the intense desire for stardom has always been LeAnn's idea. "We've never pushed her. She has pushed us and that is the truth. She came to us and said she wanted to do this," Belinda said. Wilbur and Belinda believed in their daughter one hundred percent.

Belinda adds, "I've learned in life that all people are special. But LeAnn is a very special child. I feel that she's a gift from God."

With faith, confidence, and hope in their hearts, the Rimes family headed west from Jackson, Mississippi, straight to Dallas, Texas.

CHAPTER THREE

☆ ☆ ☆

Dazzling Dallas

Dallas is as big as Pearl is small. The flatness of the land lets you see for miles in every direction. The roads are wide, the freeway entrance and exit ramps are long, and the landscape is vast. In 1841, when it was settled, Dallas was a tiny trading post on the banks of the Trinity River. Today it is the eighth-largest city in the United States and the entertainment and cultural center of the Southwest. With a little bit of country, a touch of Western, a dash of south-of-the-border mixed in with soaring skyscrapers, neon lights, and cosmopolitan centers, Dallas makes a major impression on people of all ages and backgrounds.

If LeAnn's dreams in Pearl were big, then in Dallas they would be huge.

The Rimes family's decision to move from Pearl to Dallas was based on one goal: to find more places for LeAnn to perform. Wilbur sold his coon dogs and everything else he owned. He transferred from his company's Mississippi branch to its location in Dallas. Now LeAnn was in a city that had the entertainment opportunities she would need as she took her next steps to the top.

Wilbur went to work every day. Belinda worked part-time. Each had a second full-time job: turning their talented daughter into the star she yearned to be.

Garland, Texas, where the Rimeses decided to settle, is a shining example of a solid American suburb. Garland boasts the highest percentage of married couples and home ownership in Texas. Located in northeast Dallas County, just fifteen minutes from downtown, Garland has the same geographical relationship with downtown Dallas as Pearl has with Jackson.

In Garland, home for the Rimeses was a two-bedroom apartment on East Centerville Road. A multitrack recorder and sound mixing board dominated the living room. Some families sit on the living-room couches and chairs watching TV and talking. The Rimeses did that, to be sure, but most of the time LeAnn and Wilbur worked: selecting material, arranging the songs to best feature her voice, rehearsing her performances, and recording her music. Wonder if her neighbors knew they were hearing a legend in the making!

Now that they were in Texas with the purpose of nurturing her career, LeAnn insisted that her parents take her to every opry and performance hall in the Dallas area. A tall, plainspoken man, Wilbur quickly learned what he had to do.

ADVICE FROM
DOLLY PARTON

Dolly Parton grew up in the Great Smoky Mountains of eastern Tennessee, singing through a childhood that saw equal parts hard times and pure family love. Dolly and LeAnn had the support, blessings, and encouragement of their parents to pursue their dreams of singing for others.

DOLLY TELLS LeANN:
"You have to rely on your own gut instincts and the family thing, and not lose your place and let ego or other people's flowery words pull you astray. [You] certainly [have] the gift."

LeAnn was barely seven years old. That gorgeous face and big smile were already in evidence, and she was rarin' to go. Even at six she had a lot of stage experience under her belt. Talent-show trophies, banners, certificates, and tiaras were piling up. She already had won—or would soon win—awards in both local and national Showstopper and Regency competitions and a

Miss National Imperial finalist award.

Saturday afternoon, LeAnn rehearsed her songs with Wilbur. Wilbur explained that "Crazy," the classic country song written by Willie Nelson, was a sad torch song about someone losing their love. LeAnn thought about that and the next thing you know, she was singing with soaring emotion about aspects of life she'd never experienced, singing to make you cry.

Belinda helped LeAnn select the clothes she'd wear onstage from the wardrobe that they carefully chose and paid for with their hard-earned money. Would she wear her organdy dress and anklet socks? A pair of pants with a matching top and a Stetson hat? Would her thick blond hair be piled up on her head or cascade to her shoulders?

The ride from the Rimeses' apartment to the Garland Opry at 605 State Street takes you up Broadway, right into the heart of town.

Every Saturday night, the Garland Country Music Association operates the opry. Families looking for weekend fun find plenty of music, lots of popcorn and soft drinks, and an alcohol-free setting. Kids, parents, and grandparents clap their hands, stomp their feet, sing along, or even get a few tears in their eyes as they watch some of the stars of tomorrow. Up to twelve different performers sing, dance, and play their hearts out at each Saturday-night show.

Every career has memorable turning points. For LeAnn, her audition at the Garland Opry was such a moment.

"She was so cute," Garland Opry board member Trish Freeman said. "When she finished her audition, her dad picked her up from off the stage, and she was so tiny."

LeAnn made the cut, and it wasn't long before she was scheduled to give her first live performance in the Dallas area.

The Garland Opry's show started at eight P.M., so the Rimeses left right after supper. LeAnn climbed into the backseat of the world's smallest tour bus, the family car.

Backstage in the dressing room, all of the performers and their proud mamas and papas bustled about, getting ready for that big moment. LeAnn changed into her costume for the evening, and Belinda put the finishing touches on her hair. Just a little makeup and lipstick to bring out the natural beauty of her face made certain that LeAnn would look as good on the stage as she sounded.

When her turn came, LeAnn held her head up proudly and did her show. Belinda and Wilbur stood in the wings. How nervous would you be to see your child on a stage in a theater perhaps a bit more professional than the ones she'd mastered before? Her stage presence and big voice were already tuned up, and LeAnn didn't display the least bit of stage fright. As she began to sing, LeAnn the child was instantly transformed into LeAnn the professional singer.

Her look—her hair and makeup and her clothing—was totally appropriate for her age. LeAnn's style was just right. Her desire to choose her own clothes was as intense as any six-year-old's. And Belinda's instinctive sense of hairstyling and makeup was right on target.

A picture of LeAnn at six in a puffy-sleeved dress made of the palest blue shiny fabric, with a white lace inset below the neck, says it all. The merest touch of blush on her cheeks, perfect pink lipstick, and a pink bow sweeping her hair back from her face, leaving a whisper of bangs on her forehead—well, it's about as adorable a picture as you'll ever see.

LeAnn sang her song, reveled in the applause, and triumphantly left the stage of the Garland Opry.

The Texas years in the career of LeAnn Rimes had just begun.

A few of the towns near Garland ran similar shows. The Greenville Opry and the Mesquite Opry, the Grapevine Opry and the Wylie Opry. Some operated year-round, and others were open only from spring to fall. With so many stages to play and so many slots on the bills, the Texas opry circuit was hopping every Saturday night.

That first Saturday night was easy: they played only one show. Saturday nights in the lives of LeAnn Rimes and her two beaming parents got busier after that. Wilbur booked LeAnn into several appearances each weekend. Careful timing got them to the shows on schedule. The logical "tour routing" that professional road managers employ saved the Rimeses from criss-crossing the same roads all night. Every Saturday night, Wilbur and Belinda drove LeAnn from one show to another, multiplying the number of people she turned into instant fans.

"She'd be sleeping in the car as we drove to the next opry," says Belinda, "and then she'd get up on the stage and sing 'Crazy' and then get right back in the car and go to sleep."

Sundays they'd go to church and hope to catch a

little relaxation before work and school rolled around
again.

But a seven-year-old—even one with a blooming
musical career—needs to have more than a nightlife.
Wilbur and Belinda weren't about to let the rest of
LeAnn's development be sacrificed for her singing. An
education was important to them.

There are about sixty schools in the Garland
Independent School District, the second-largest school
district in Dallas County. Garland's innovative Freedom
of Choice plan means schools have no "attendance
zones," allowing the town's forty-four thousand students
the flexibility to choose from campuses across the district, rather than being limited to their neighborhood
school.

Entering Club Hill Elementary School as a second
grader, LeAnn continued her studies with the same
commitment and enthusiasm that had earned her a place
on the Pearl Lower Elementary School honor roll. Even
though she could sing like no other child in her class,
she fit right in and easily made the adjustments to a new
school.

In the phys. ed. program at Club Hill Elementary and in
Garland's many excellent recreational facilities, LeAnn
participated in softball and swimming, both of which she
loved.

Listening to Broadway show tunes inspired LeAnn to
dream about acting and singing in a musical. Remember,
she had won her first big talent contest in Flowood with
"Getting to Know You" from *The King and I*. After her
godparents gave her the soundtrack to *Cats*, she won

more contests singing "Memories." In 1989, when she was seven, LeAnn made her stage debut in a Dallas musical production of *A Christmas Carol,* playing the role of Tiny Tim, one of the leads.

That was also the year she learned to yodel.

The town of Mesquite, east of Dallas, is home to the world famous Mesquite Championship Rodeo. In May 1958, seven young cowboys got together and realized there was plenty of demand and a big potential audience for a weekly rodeo. Weekly competitions have been held ever since.

Regular features include the always dangerous bull riding, daredevil clowns, high-flying broncs, sharpshooting calf ropers, brawny steer wrestlers, and pretty barrel racers. Rodeo bulls with names such as Mad Dog, Exorcist, and Final Countdown give the crowd—made up of locals, newcomers to the area, and domestic and foreign visitors—enough thrills each Friday and Saturday night to last the whole week.

The Mesquite Opry was one of LeAnn's regular Saturday-night stops. Now she was going to ride in the opry's float in the Mesquite Championship Rodeo Parade, an annual icing-on-the-cake event that turned the whole town into one big party.

The Mesquite Opry was run by Janet McBride and her husband. As Janet and LeAnn sat together under a tree and waited for the opry's float to be placed in line for the parade, LeAnn told the older woman she wanted to learn to yodel, and Janet, who happened to be a good yodeler herself, said okay.

Janet yodeled and explained a few techniques to her

young friend. For the next two hours, they practiced. LeAnn caught on as quickly as she always did when she wanted to master a new skill.

Later that afternoon, the beautiful Mesquite Opry float, bearing the equally beautiful LeAnn, arrived at the crowded town square. There LeAnn stood, smiling sweetly as she sang "I Want to Be a Cowboy's Sweetheart." The song, first recorded in 1935, is believed to be the first million-selling hit recorded by a female country artist. Patsy Montana, born and raised in Arkansas, was a female pioneer in country music. She helped create the yodeling-cowgirl image that Patsy Cline adopted and that LeAnn had fallen in love with, too.

By the time the float moved within sight of Belinda and Wilbur, LeAnn was yodeling like she'd grown up in the Swiss Alps. Her parents could only stare in amazement—and not for the first time—at their remarkable child.

Wilbur and Belinda sat in the darkened theater on Broadway in New York City and watched their eight-year-old-daughter audition for the lead in *Annie 2*, the follow-up to one of the biggest musicals of all time. Scores of talented girls fidgeted and fussed and giggled as they waited their turns. Like every other anxious mom and dad in the theater, the Rimeses hoped their child would impress the producers.

LeAnn sang "Happy Birthday," in a rendition totally her own. She was one of eleven kids asked to return for the final call. When the part went to a twelve-year-old, LeAnn was philosophical. "They thought I was too young to carry the show."

After spending a week in New York for the *Annie 2* audition, Belinda thought that LeAnn should focus on the world of country music. "Baby, we can't be flying back and forth to New York every time there's a tryout for a Broadway show," she said. "Maybe we can go through the good, clean country venues and see what happens."

The Lyndon B. Johnson Freeway makes a circle around Dallas and through Garland on Interstates 20 and 635. It takes you from Garland to Fort Worth.

The Rimeses were driving toward a high school auditorium in Fort Worth, the current home of Johnnie High's Country Music Revue. From a variety of locations in the Dallas/Fort Worth area and for nearly two decades, Johnnie High's had been the largest and most successful of the area's many amateur opries. Johnnie High's had launched the careers of country singing stars Gary Morris and Linda Davis, among many others.

Fort Worth is a beautiful city. Its old red-brick streets, beautiful flower beds, and grand historic buildings, including the pink granite Tarrant County Courthouse, sit beneath towering glass-and-steel skyscrapers. It has a wonderful cultural district with enough museums, galleries, and artistic and musical events to make it a top contender on any list of great cities.

Fort Worth earned its nickname, Cowtown, for all the cows and steers who arrived (along with plenty of strapping cowboys) at the last stop on the old Chisholm Trail. The Cowtown Coliseum, built in 1907, came soon after the establishment of the Stockyards Museum in 1904. Near both is the Stockyards Hotel, where Bonnie and

Clyde reportedly took a rest between robberies.

Country music and Western traditions are the heart and soul of Fort Worth, making it a great location for Johnnie High. The music at Johnnie High's is always top-notch, thanks to Johnnie's great ear and the terrific family-entertainment atmosphere created by his wife, Wanda. High's mission is to nurture talented youngsters, give them a place to bloom, and send them on their way.

"The fun to me is watching them grow and mature," High said. "They're like little birds leaving the nest."

From the stage that had seen many great moments before her, as well as countless assemblies, school plays, and choir performances, LeAnn sang "Crazy" and "Blue Moon of Kentucky" in her audition for Johnnie High. At six feet, three inches, wearing a bright red jacket, he may have seemed like a giant to this little girl so eager to get her chance on his stage, but his big smile and kind eyes quickly put her at ease.

"She created sparks that day. She was special," he said. Johnnie High began his musical career when he was fifteen and has spent his share of time on stages large and small as a musician with country legends such as Ernest Tubb and Eddy Arnold. He said he got goose bumps listening to LeAnn sing.

"She had poise, dedication, and stage presence. She didn't look like a pageant girl. She looked like a country singer and she just come out and done it," he said.

A couple of Saturdays later, LeAnn rehearsed with Wilbur for about two and a half hours. She and Belinda took extra care in choosing an outfit to mark this occasion as truly special. When they arrived at the Fort Worth auditorium, they finished up in the dressing room back-stage.

LeAnn walked out onstage and started singing.

"She brought down the house," Johnnie said.

From that night on, LeAnn spent almost every Saturday night at Johnnie High's, singing country-and-western classics. Soon, LeAnn was as comfortable at Johnnie High's as any professional musician. And, like every pro, she continued to prepare herself for each show vigorously and carefully.

It wasn't long before LeAnn found herself in the best slot on the program—the last, closing the show to a standing ovation every week.

"It taught LeAnn a whole bunch to be on his show," Wilbur says. "It was great for her and it's been great for a lot of other kids in Texas."

Some nights, she took a nap before performing. Or, before and after rehearsing, she played with Wanda and Johnnie's granddaughter in a game room backstage. Like all kids, she enjoyed Barbie dolls and other games. But when she went onstage, she was entirely different.

"The audience was in awe of her and so was every-body else," says High. "Some people just have an aura about them, so you know they're in the room. Little kids wanted to dress like her, and the eighty-year-olds were crazy about her, too."

Patsy Montana came to see LeAnn at Johnnie High's. Posing together backstage for a photographer, they wore the same smile, the one that shows the joy of singing and making people happy.

"She was a professional every time she went on,"

High says. "She never forgot a word or messed up once. She was perfection onstage."

The two thousand members of Johnnie High's Country Music Revue Association voted LeAnn Rimes the Best Act Under 16.

And the proud parents were also gaining fans. Wilbur had invested his life and all his resources into LeAnn's career. Those who knew Belinda considered her one of the sweetest, nicest, most Christian women on earth. She had devoted her life to her child, especially to making sure her unusual gift wouldn't have any unwelcome consequences.

Belinda believed that LeAnn was born to "touch hearts . . . through her voice. I don't know where it's going to end, but I know she's here for a purpose. People come up to me and say it's not normal that she sings like that and I say I know it isn't. It's a God-given talent."

Over the next six years, LeAnn performed more than three hundred consecutive Saturday nights at Johnnie High's Country Music Revue.

Working every Saturday night and devoting hours of practice each week to her music didn't leave LeAnn with a lot of time for the typical activities of an eight-year-old. How many eight-year-olds spend their time making demo tapes with their dads? She got along well with her classmates at Club Hill Elementary and had a few close friends. But she missed the slumber parties, movie dates, and other things kids did together. She did make time for softball.

In a coed Little League softball match when she was

eight, LeAnn stepped up to the plate and hit a home run clear over the outfielder's head. One little boy was amazed. His mouth was hanging open and his eyes were "this wide," according to Wilbur, who then heard the little boy say, "Girls ain't supposed to do that!" You're wrong, kid, especially about this girl.

Two or three times a week, LeAnn and her third-grade classmates attended Mrs. Armas's music class for a thirty-minute session. They sang or played musical instruments and games. Music class was required for all the students at Club Hill Elementary School.

Mrs. Trudy Armas, Club Hill's music teacher and choir director, had worked with hundreds of children. LeAnn's talent wasn't all that impressed her.

"She was a really pretty, smart, quiet, and cooperative girl and could sing real good. But she didn't sing with her stage voice in class," Mrs. Armas said. "She blended right in. When she got to her talent shows, then she sang in her stage voice. But it was not the type of singing to do in class." LeAnn knew that.

The other kids didn't resent their talented classmate who sang all over town on Saturday nights.

When she was chosen for the lead in the 1990 Club Elementary Christmas program, LeAnn rehearsed with the cast several times a week. But Mrs. Armas had to find a stand-in for the night of the performance. LeAnn was out of town.

Talent shows. Softball games. Conquering every stage on the Dallas opry circuit. Standing ovations at least once a week. A lead role in the school play, not to mention in a Dallas musical. Nearly reprising *Annie*, one of the greatest child-star-making parts in the history of Broadway. What new world would she conquer next? Well, as it turns out, the biggest arena of them all—television.

The aspiring young performers waited their turns to impress a panel of producers and talent agents. Each listened as a beautiful model read the rules of the competition. All had carefully prepared the programs that made them shine in their particular categories: female vocalist, male vocalist, musical group, stand-up comedian, dance, dramatic, and TV spokesmodel.

LeAnn had decided to sing the Marty Robbins song "Don't Worry About Me" in the Best Female Vocalist category. For the first time in a long time, she had butterflies in her stomach. But when she went out onstage, the fear disappeared. Her performance was so smashing, she was invited back for another round of a contest that could ultimately lead to a prize of one hundred thousand dollars.

The show was *Star Search*, a syndicated sixty-minute TV extravaganza hosted by the one and only Ed McMahon. It launched many a show-business career in the 1980s. Could it do for LeAnn what *Arthur Godfrey's Talent Scouts* had done for Patsy Cline back in the fifties?

LeAnn's second round of competition was, unfortunately, her last. Did that second panel of judges have cotton in their ears?

The shows she'd taped around Christmas were broadcast the following April. By then LeAnn had gone on to many other things.

* * *

Everyone who heard LeAnn sing at Johnnie High's was totally amazed. One person who'd seen her called Marty Rendelman, who runs a celebrity-related business in the Dallas area and knows a lot of people in the music business.

Rendelman's friend told her, "There's this incredibly talented little girl, and the family is really sweet. Some shyster is going to come along and take advantage. Would you see if you can help in any way?"

Rendelman then went to see LeAnn and had the same reaction everyone else did. Later, Rendelman called Tanya Tucker's father, Beau, who had guided his daughter's career.

"He gave me about sixteen reasons to run like hell," she said. "Kids can't sign contracts, you can't work them all over the place, they have to go to school, you have child labor laws, you need a tour bus, and they all come with parents, one of whom is usually a stage mom."

In the beginning, as Wilbur knew so well, a manager is also a booking agent, career consultant and developer, publicist, image consultant, and everything else the artist needs. All this for no money. It's a thankless job and you work for a very long time before seeing any results, if you ever do.

"You have to be crazy," Rendelman says, "or believe you can create something great."

Well, Rendelman did agree to work with LeAnn and her parents. As she joked to LeAnn, "I spent the first six months trying to get rid of you." She called producers and record-company executives in New York and Los Angeles for advice on who might want to work with a child with the most incredible voice. She sent them tapes, and though many agreed that in LeAnn's voice they heard the quality Rendelman was talking about, nobody jumped on board to sign LeAnn to a record deal.

Still, Rendelman felt she could do some things to help LeAnn. "She was in many ways a typical nine-year-old, but being an only child, she was more mature. She made good grades in school and was a very sweet young girl."

Obviously, LeAnn was too young to play in any music clubs where liquor was sold. So Rendelman booked her on what would be the first of many dates singing the National Anthem.

The night of the concert at the Walt Garrison Rodeo, LeAnn had a sore throat. The soundman didn't show up, so the band couldn't play. Not to worry: LeAnn sang the anthem a cappella.

"That was the turning point," Ms. Rendelman said. "Everybody just fell over dead, this ten-year-old singing a cappella."

One of the people there was Verna Riddles, Troy Aikman's manager, who called soon after to book LeAnn for an Aikman Foundation benefit.

One successful appearance always led to another. Thousands of Texans will tell you they saw the nine-, then ten-, then eleven-year-old LeAnn sing America's biggest hit song, "The Star-Spangled Banner." That's because LeAnn Rimes singing the National Anthem was a regular feature at home games in sports-loving Dallas. At a Dallas Cowboys game in Texas Stadium. At Reunion Arena, kicking off a Dallas Sidekicks soccer game or making a slam dunk with the Dallas Mavericks. LeAnn sang for the Texas Rangers in both

Arlington Stadium and at the Ballpark.

LeAnn played at all the opries in Dallas, Fort Worth, Waco, and Houston. She'd gone east to Branson, Missouri, and played several places, and then farther east to Nashville to play at Opryland and Gilley's. She even went back to Mississippi to play Pearl Day.

Marty Rendelman continued to tell anyone who would listen, "There hasn't been a Shirley Temple or a Judy Garland in a lot of years. If someone with some creativity and some promotional skills saw what I see in the way of the voice, the face, the sweetness, even the brains—it's the total package, the real deal. And it doesn't come along very often."

Publicity pictures of LeAnn from back then show her looking "too cool for school," as they say. A close-up, smiling brightly with a black Stetson tipped back on her head, or a full-length pose in a light Western suit with gold trim, both show a girl who looks like she knows exactly where she's going.

Her bio sheet proclaims: "The future star of country music has arrived."

Sitting with her classmates early one morning in the fifth-grade classroom of Mrs. Norma Nix, LeAnn was told she'd had a phone call. It was President George Bush calling to ask if she could leave school immediately to sing at the opening of a large manufacturing plant nearby. The principal asked Mrs. Nix if LeAnn could be dismissed at about nine A.M. Off she went with the president, and she didn't return to school for the rest of the day. And it wasn't the only time LeAnn missed school to perform.

"She'd call later for assignments," Mrs. Nix said. "She made up every bit of the work. She'd stay in to catch up on an art project. You could see these traits forming at an early age. The determination And of course, her talent. You could hear her potential."

Because she maintained all A's and B's in the fourth and fifth grades, LeAnn was allowed to try out for the school's honors-level choir. (She made it, by the way.) Mrs. Armas made all the fourth graders sopranos and the fifth graders altos, there being a scarcity of tenors and basses among her nine- and ten-year-olds. About ninety boys and girls met once or twice a week for practice. They practiced more often when they had a date to sing for the Lions Club, the Rotary Club, the Junior League, or another community event. The choir sang to tapes or was accompanied by a pianist. Sometimes they sang a cappella, and LeAnn was frequently a featured soloist.

When Jocelyn White, at the time an entertainment reporter in Dallas, brought a channel 4 TV camera crew to Club Hill Elementary to interview LeAnn, the fifth grader took it all in stride. She even helped her classmates to feel more at ease during the taping. Why not? She'd already been on several Dallas-area talk shows as well as national television.

LeAnn concentrated on music and dance. She practiced gymnastics, according to Mrs. Nix, "to make her better on the stage."

Mrs. Nix thought the world of LeAnn. "With all the attention she was getting, she amazed me. She was never the spoiled child. It could have gone to her head, but she was mature and handled herself well. At the age of ten, it was a lot to handle."

Singing everywhere she could, LeAnn joined the Garland All-City Girls Choir, making her just about the busiest fifth grader in town.

The commitment and devotion of Wilbur and Belinda Rimes impressed everyone at the school. "They sacrificed every bit of the way. They never pressured her. They are very down-home folks with old-fashioned morals and beliefs," Mrs. Nix said. "It was hard on her mom; she did without a lot. Expensive recording sessions, the right type of clothes . . . they were willing to do it as long as she wanted it."

Most of LeAnn's classmates just loved her and enjoyed all the attention she brought to their school. But not all of them. "Some of the kids got jealous," Mrs. Nix said, "but we treated her the same way as everyone else. We never made a big ado about it."

LeAnn dealt calmly with everything that was going on in her preteen life, according to her fifth-grade teacher. "She made the decisions. She was never wishy-washy about her future. She always knew. A remarkable young lady."

This "remarkable young lady" continued her Saturday-night appearances at Johnnie High's. Meanwhile, Marty Rendelman continued to find the fairs, festivals, and convention work that expanded LeAnn's local audience. Wilbur continued to tell people who praised his daughter, "She's just got a gift. She came here with it."

Going to see other performers in concert taught LeAnn more and more about how to please an audience. Though her singing always dazzled the crowds, she was less comfortable with talking to the audience between songs. She was never shy, but her instrument wasn't her talking voice, it was definitely her singing voice.

Sometimes, LeAnn's "Star-Spangled Banner" singing engagements were scheduled at eight or nine in the morning. Because Belinda and Wilbur worked, at such times LeAnn would spend the night before at Marty Rendelman's house. Marty's daughter was a big sister to LeAnn, a special treat for this only child.

Referring to one of these engagements, Rendelman tells this story: "We were driving back from the function, sitting in a line of traffic at a tollbooth and LeAnn was rubbing her eyes. She said, 'Don't book me this early.' I told her, 'Look, you already made a hundred and fifty dollars this morning and now we're going out to breakfast. You see all those people? They're driving to jobs they probably hate. We're the lucky ones.' "

Where did Marty Rendelman think LeAnn got her talent? She answered without hesitation, "From Wilbur. With every gifted child, one parent has a talent. Those genes are inherited. If it happens without the genes, then that's the miracle. Wilbur Rimes can sing, but he's too embarrassed and he could never get up onstage. He has perfect pitch, and that's why LeAnn sounds so good. I relied on Wilbur a lot. I said, 'The business end is mine, but the note is your responsibility.'"

LeAnn continued to listen to as much music as she could. Every great singer and musician has stacks of records and cassettes and CDs. Painters visit museums, authors read lots of books, actors go to the theater and to movies, and athletes analyze each other's moves. Where else can you learn than from the ones you admire most in your field?

Adding Whitney Houston to her list of favorite singers was only natural after LeAnn heard Whitney's unbelievable voice. And in 1992, when *The Bodyguard* came out, the story of a singing star's life onstage and off with the man who is sworn to protect her became one of LeAnn's favorite movies.

Back in Pearl, Mississippi, the Rimes family was thrilled with news coming in from Texas. They were all rooting for LeAnn.

So was Beverly Smith, who frequently ran into Thad Butler. One day she stopped in at Butler's Portable Buildings on Highway 80. "I'll tell you what, I went down there to buy one of those buildings and he had a tape of LeAnn singing somewhere in Texas and he wanted to give it to me . . . he was telling me then that she was doing so great but I hear that so much that I just kind of shrug it off, it's just another parent who thinks their child is great."

LeAnn reached her eleventh birthday in August 1993 and, a few weeks later, entered the sixth grade at Brandenburg Middle School in Garland. She continued her singing with the school choir and the Garland All-City Girls Choir, but her schedule was taking her out of town more and more often. As in Club Hill, she was required to make up any work she missed. According to Carol Hartman, who works at Brandenburg, "Some students make up their work without hesitation. LeAnn was one of these students."

Belinda, Wilbur, and LeAnn all felt terrific, and why not? They had come to Texas, and they all had devoted themselves to LeAnn's dream. She had made real progress, lots of friends and fans, and even some headlines in a city that knows the difference between great musical performers and amateurs.

A friend of the Rimeses' in Fort Worth set up an audition for LeAnn with Jimmy Bowen, one of the most successful record producers and industry executives in popular music. At the time, Bowen was the owner and head of Liberty Records, whose biggest recording artist—anyone's biggest recording artist—was Garth Brooks.

Even more amazing than Jimmy Bowen agreeing to hear LeAnn Rimes was the story of how Bowen had made his first record. He had attended West Texas College in Canyon, Texas, and in 1955 played in a country-turned-rockabilly band. He visited Norman Petty's recording studio in Clovis, New Mexico (remember that name), and persuaded Petty to let them record some music. By 1957, that session had led to sales of more than a million records.

The Rimeses journeyed to Nashville to meet with Bowen. LeAnn sang two songs for Bowen in his living room.

Bowen thought she was great and told her so. "Your voice is six or seven years ahead of where it should be," he said. "I have to tell you, though, I don't sign children."

Glad that Bowen had praised her vocal skills and seemed impressed with her talent, LeAnn said, "He told me he didn't sign kids, because he didn't believe in putting them on the road but for me to come back when I'm eighteen."

LeAnn had already been singing for half her life. Did she really have to wait another six years to get her chance to break into the big time? "I know I was kinda ready then," she said, "but I wasn't really. He was right to tell me to wait, but I wanted it."

CHAPTER FOUR

☆ ☆ ☆

Starbound

Nashville wasn't ready for LeAnn, but back in
Garland, she was still the town's best-known young
woman. Most people were on her side, in her corner,
cheering her on and hoping she'd one day have the kind
of success she so richly deserved.

In her black Stetson and chaps, LeAnn sat tall and
proud, looking like a professional horsewoman at the
Celebrity Cutting Horse Contest sponsored by the
Mesquite Rodeo at Texas Stadium. Bred to "cut" into
herds of cattle, cutting horses move quickly and grace-
fully. Mesquite Rodeo announcer James Jennings, who
worked the show, said LeAnn was "tickled to death" to
be at the event, and was a great rider to boot.

Jennings also watched as LeAnn sang the National
Anthem for a professional bull-riding show in Texas
Stadium. "I found her to be just who she is," Jennings
said, "not pretentious, not patent leather. And an unbelievable voice."

It had been many years since he'd been so moved by
a singer, Jennings said. When he went to announce a
rodeo in Oklahoma, he was told that the singer of the

National Anthem at that event was a young girl nobody had ever really heard of. "Her voice was just unreal," Jennings said. "Here was this skinny, freckle-faced kid with an unbelievable voice. Not only that, like LeAnn, she could really use that voice well.

"That girl," Jennings added with a chuckle, "was Reba McEntire."

Most of the students at Club Hill were a hundred percent behind LeAnn, but a few others started giving her trouble.

"I had a lot of friends, but there were these [kids] who were scaring me sometimes. They egged my locker the last day of school," LeAnn explained. "My mom had to pick me up an hour after school started. People were threatening to beat me up. And they would have done that . . . and I'm sitting here in an apartment going, 'What am I doing wrong?' It's like [they think], 'You're rich now,' and I'm like, 'Oh yeah, I really am.'

"I was different from everybody because a lot of people didn't understand what I did," she says. "I'm like, 'I'm just normal, like everybody else.' I think that's an important thing these days, to let everybody know you're normal. I might have one quality they don't have—I can sing—and they might have one that I don't."

Solving those problems—plus an increasingly busy travel schedule that interfered with school—required some clear thinking. Committed as they were to their daughter's education, Wilbur and Belinda had to ask themselves, How could LeAnn have a normal eleven-year-old's life when her pursuit of stardom and what it took to attain it made her life anything but normal?

"It's going to be hard for her to be in class every day, because she'll be doing a lot of traveling," Marty Rendelman said. "But there's a trade-off. She'll see a lot of places and meet a lot of people."

One of the people LeAnn met was attorney Lyle Walker.

Continuing her schedule of appearances at corporate functions, fairs, clubs, stadiums and sports arenas, festivals, parties, and opries—everywhere, in short, but nightclubs, where it was illegal for her to play—she kept her eye on her dream.

She also continued her regular Saturday-night gig in Fort Worth at Johnnie High's.

The night Lyle Walker heard LeAnn, he was completely blown away.

"I felt she had the most amazing voice I'd ever heard," he said. "A once-in-a-lifetime talent. I told her what she needed was an album."

Now, a lot of people had that very same idea after seeing LeAnn perform. But Lyle Walker was different: He owned a recording studio, and he offered to put up the money to make LeAnn's first album.

Bill Mack, the Midnight Cowboy, is a legendary disc jockey on Dallas radio station WBAP-AM in Arlington and a longtime resident of Fort Worth. He wrote his first song when he was eleven years old; hundreds more followed, many of which he never even bothered to keep. He knew his way around a song. He'd also heard plenty of great music of all kinds sung by gifted singers of all ages in his decades as a DJ.

So what did he say after he heard a tape of eleven-year-old LeAnn Rimes singing "The Star-Spangled Banner"?

From under his black Stetson, Bill Mack's eyes look right at you so piercingly and full of smiles that it's startling. "I'm not exaggerating," he said. "The hair stood up on my arm. I forgot all about her age. You just don't hear anybody sing 'The Star-Spangled Banner' that good."

LeAnn has commented that the National Anthem is a hard song to sing. "I do the Whitney Houston version," she says.

Mack was captivated by the emotional grit and from-the-gut honesty in LeAnn's voice. "At eleven years old, it was frightening how unbelievably good she was," he said. Then he had a great idea.

In 1959, Bill Mack was a skinny DJ making $135 a week at a small radio station in Wichita Falls. One day he composed a five-chord ballad on his guitar. "I wrote the song in a matter of fifteen minutes. I thought it was an awfully simple song."

He recorded it himself as the B-side of a single in 1960, but nothing much came of it. At the time, Patsy Cline was at the height of her popularity, and a friend thought Bill might want to pitch it to her. When Patsy's husband, Charlie Dick, heard the tape, he agreed it would be perfect for Patsy.

But Patsy never got around to recording the song; she died tragically in a plane crash in 1963. Bill Mack just held on to the song . . . until he heard LeAnn Rimes. Or, as he says, "Until I found the voice I wanted to hear sing it."

The song was "Blue."

WHO WAS PATSY CLINE?

Patsy Cline, born in Winchester, Virginia, in 1932, is considered one of the most important female country artists of all time. In 1973 she became the first female performer to be elected to the Country Music Hall of Fame, and today, more than three decades after her death, her records continue to sell in the millions each year.

As a child, Patsy sang along with WSM radio's broadcasts of the Grand Ole Opry. She won a local tap-dance competition at the age of four and went on to sing in school plays and the church choir. At eight, she taught herself to play the piano. At thirteen, she sang in a dance hall with a band, and at fourteen she sang on a local radio station. She dropped out of school in her mid-teens and helped support her family by singing in local taverns, beer joints, racetracks, and family clubs while also working in a drugstore.

Patsy claimed right from the start that she knew she would someday be a star. Her mother, who was only sixteen years older than Patsy, had complete faith in her talent, independence, and determined spirit. Together they came to Nashville for the first time in 1947. At sixteen, Patsy sang all over town for many of the people who would go on to help her realize her dream. She impressed everyone with her magical combination of quiet self-confidence and a rich, powerful voice. At five feet, ten inches tall, she was a true presence.

After landing a record deal, she recorded four singles that went nowhere. Then Patsy was persuaded to record a song, "Walkin' After Midnight," that had originally been written for her favorite pop singer, Kay Starr, but had been rejected by Starr's record label. When she sang the song on *Arthur Godfrey's Talent Scouts* on national TV the evening of January 21, 1957, she wore a cocktail dress instead of her usual cowgirl outfit. The single reached number three on the country charts and landed in the top fifteen of the pop charts.

Over the next few years, Patsy Cline won the hearts of music lovers of all ages with such country and pop crossover hits as "Crazy" and "I Fall to Pieces," her first number one. In 1961, she was inducted into the Grand Ole Opry, one of the highest honors a country musician can attain.

On March 5, 1963, returning to Nashville from a benefit concert in Kansas City, Patsy Cline was killed in a plane crash, along with her manager, Randy Hughes, and fellow musicians the Country Copas and Hawkshaw Hawkins.

The 1980 film biography of Loretta Lynn, *Coal Miner's Daughter,* touched on

Patsy Cline's life. A few years later, Cline herself was the main character, portrayed stunningly by Jessica Lange, in the movie *Sweet Dreams*. Both movies revived interest in Patsy Cline, and by 1993 there were more than fifty Patsy Cline albums on fourteen different record labels.

Patsy Cline's voice lives on as it influences the work of everyone from Loretta Lynn to Reba McEntire to LeAnn Rimes and inspires the hearts of millions who continue to listen to her.

"My dad heard the tape and threw it in the corner," LeAnn said. "He thought it was too old for me. But I kept bugging him about it. I stuck it back in the tape recorder and said, 'I love that.'"

Wilbur took a little longer to be convinced. "The first time I heard 'Blue' I didn't like it, but it was a demo version that sounded old-fashioned."

"At first we didn't know that it was for Patsy Cline," LeAnn said.

LeAnn kept thinking about the song. She had always sung old-fashioned songs, and many of them were mature for someone her age. Wilbur simply explained the lyrics to her and she took it from there.

"Like an actress interpreting a script, I'm an interpreter of a song," LeAnn says. "I know what the songs are all about, though I haven't lived it yet." There's a youthful purity in her voice along with the sense that she really understands all the infidelities and heart-breaks she sings about.

"I knew 'Blue' was perfect for me," she said. "Then I got the idea to put that little yodel thing to it."

One afternoon when Wilbur came home, LeAnn said, "Daddy, listen to this."

Wilbur listened.

"LeAnn added the yodel and then I fell in love with it," he said. "She really transformed the song." Wilbur agreed LeAnn could add "Blue" to her song list.

Bill Mack says he "had never been more taken or enthused over an artist. When I first saw LeAnn, I thought she was the greatest I had ever seen. Talk about way ahead of your time."

Lyle Walker owned Norman Petty Studios in Clovis, New Mexico. The very same place where Jimmy Bowen had made that surprise million seller back in the fifties, it was also where music legends Buddy Holly and Roy Orbison had recorded some of their early hits.

"I actually sang on the microphone Buddy Holly used," said LeAnn. "That was a thrill."

Over three successive weekends in the spring of 1994, LeAnn, Wilbur, Belinda, and Marty Rendelman crossed the Texas border to Clovis in the easternmost part of New Mexico.

"LeAnn was so excited because she was recording the songs she liked most of all," Belinda said.

If LeAnn was at home on the stage, in the studio she was a natural. "She came in and did most of the songs in

one take, sang them her own way," Lyle Walker said.
Wilbur produced the album with Johnny Mulhair,
assisted by Greg Walker.

Of course, LeAnn recorded "Blue" in one take.
Singing Dolly Parton's "I Will Always Love You" in
the studio enabled LeAnn to add even more vocal gymnastics to a song she often sang onstage. LeAnn also sang
the Beatles' "Yesterday" and one of her oldest favorites,
Patsy Montana's "I Want to Be a Cowboy's Sweetheart."

Marty Rendelman wanted LeAnn and Wilbur to sing
a duet for the album, but Wilbur said no. "Wilbur's perfect pitch is part of why LeAnn sounds perfect,"
Rendelman said. "It can also drive the sound people
crazy."

"Sure Thing," written by Joyce Harrison, "The Rest
Is History," by Clay Blaker and Karen Staley, as well as
"Why Can't We," by Allen Shamblin, Austin
Cunningham, and Chuck Cannon, display LeAnn's
vocal talents as if the songs had been written expressly
for her. In "Broken Wing," by David Nowlen and
"Middle Man," by David Patillo, LeAnn proves she real-
ly did listen carefully to Barbra Streisand and Celine Dion.
"I'll Get Even with You," by Coweta House, is amazing.

LeAnn's "big sister," Marty Rendelman's daughter,
tried to help her keep her head on straight in the midst of
recording her first studio album at age eleven. After the
sessions in Clovis were over, she said to LeAnn,
"Girlfriend, you ain't all that!" LeAnn jumped up and
said, "That's it! That's the title of the album."

All That was released in July 1994. The cover repro-
duced a publicity shot of LeAnn smiling in her sharp

Western suit. Rendelman handled publicity, and Wilbur and Belinda visited Dallas/Fort Worth record stores to find out how to sell the record. (Talk about a mom-and-pop operation.)

The album was well received and went on to sell more than fifteen thousand copies in the Dallas/Fort Worth area alone.

"The key is to make your talent, not your age, your most important attribute and LeAnn does that splendidly," wrote pop-music critic Michael Corcoran in the *Dallas Morning News*. "LeAnn doesn't sound like any age; she just sounds good."

Corcoran also praised the album's "great vocal moments and surprisingly big-league sound."

Lyle Walker was pleased. "It's frightening if she gets any better. And she'll get better every year."

Bill Mack heard LeAnn's recording of "Blue." He said, "She did it exactly the way I wanted it done."

What about that yodel? "People call what she does with her voice a yodel, but it's not like some Swiss yodeler, it's what we call a soul break," Bill Mack said. "It's like something's tuggin' at you."

Among the people to whom LeAnn gave a copy of *All That* was Mrs. Norma Nix, her fifth-grade teacher.

LeAnn was sitting with Belinda, waiting for her turn on the stage at one of the most beautiful natural amphitheaters in the Southwest. Winter's Amphitheater, with its pecan trees, an oak grove, and a creek running through it, was the setting for the Garland Spring Creek Festival.

"This must be what outdoor concerts in heaven are like," raved the *Dallas Morning News.*

Sponsored by the Garland City Council until it could become self-supporting, the festival aimed to blend sever al art forms to attract a wide range of people. This gave audiences the chance to see, for example, the Fort Worth Ballet wearing Western costumes as they danced on pointe in a number they staged with the Dixie Chicks. The festival offered local nonprofit organizations a chance to raise money by running the food concessions. No alcohol was served.

Before performing, LeAnn told a local reporter, "I'm going to be a huge star. I want to be as big as Barbra Streisand."

Then she went onstage and, like every artist on a promotional tour, sang several songs from her new album.

Jaime Ratliff, Garland's mayor, said, "There's no way I believed she was only eleven. But look, she's just a little tiny thing up there onstage all by herself."

LeAnn did not return to Brandenburg Middle School for the seventh grade.

"Right now, I'm concentrating on singing," LeAnn said. "If I start now, then like when I'm eighteen or whatever, I could go on to college. I've always thought if I ever lost my voice, I'd teach or even be a manager or something like that."

Marty Rendelman said, "We took LeAnn to Texas Tech and Texas University, which have high school extension courses. You go for two hours a day, get homework, and then bring it back the next day, or a few days later if you're away. At least there was a monitoring process. I still tell any children I work with that they must have an education."

Home schooling is the way between 750,000 and 1.2 million U.S. kids are educated. According to CNN legal analysts Roger Cossack and Greta Van Susteren in their *The Law* column published in *USA Weekend,* there's even a Home School Legal Defense Association that helps ensure that it all goes well. Home schooling is legal in every state, and most states have set up specific curriculum requirements.

Always a conscientious and hardworking student, LeAnn teased Rendelman's daughter before she started the home schooling. "Why do I have to study? I'm going to be rich and famous one day." Seconds later, LeAnn heard this smart reply: "You're going to be asked to dine with presidents and kings. If you don't have command of the English language and good grammar, you won't achieve a thing."

"At least once a month I talk to LeAnn to reassure in my heart that this is what she wants to do," Belinda said. "She may wake up in a year or two and say, 'I don't want to do this anymore.' That's why I want her to have a good, stable education, because you can lose your voice, you may fall in love, you may decide to go down a different avenue."

One development made everyone feel a bit more confident about this big change in LeAnn's life. Tested just before she would have entered seventh grade, her skills were found to be at the ninth-grade level.

Now LeAnn was even more focused than before on becoming a full-time professional musical artist. She continued her engagements, her practicing, and her publicity. For all her star quality onstage, she was modest offstage. In interviews with the press, she revealed she didn't like her performances on tape. "I don't think anybody does," LeAnn says. "Whitney Houston was talking on TV, and she does not like to watch herself."

LeAnn was also getting tired of the big fuss over her youth. "I'm trying to make them leave my age out of it," she said. "It sounds like I'm a little kid going up there and singing." She had just turned twelve years old.

And because she was twelve, she and Belinda were starting to have those universal mother-daughter arguments about clothes. "My stage clothes are okay," LeAnn said, "but my day clothes, we cannot agree on anything."

LeAnn was keeping up with her home schooling and said she didn't really miss middle school. "I kinda miss my friends, but basically I still see them, anyway. I play baseball and softball and go swimming. My parents, they make sure I have time to do things."

On October 17, 1994, two gentlemen from Nashville sat in the audience at the refurbished Park Cities Playhouse, newly named for its location in University Park, not too far from Dallas. The lovely Art Deco theater accommodates about three hundred people and was filled to capacity for that night's show with LeAnn Rimes.

Record executives Jimmy Gilmer of EMI and Mark

Wright of Decca were knocked out by what they heard. "Their eyes were glazed over. They didn't believe it," Marty Rendelman said. "They told me, we can't tell people in Nashville about this. They won't believe it unless they see it. You have to do it again." So Rendelman arranged another appearance in January.

In both Nashville and Dallas, any night in January is prime time for an ice storm. Roads in the city may turn to sheets of black ice, and nobody goes anywhere. The first piece of good fortune the night of LeAnn's second show at the Park Cities Playhouse was that no ice storm occurred.

But backstage, there was a tornado of excitement. In a little dressing room, Wilbur, Belinda, Marty Rendelman, an image and talent consultant named Jayne Lybrand, and a professional hair and makeup artist were generating, in the words of a local reporter, "enough nervous energy to wire the sound system, if not the singer."

As the finishing touches were put on LeAnn's hair, Marty Rendelman said, "I get a little nervous, but Mama gets real nervous."

LeAnn was wearing black denim jeans, a starched white shirt, and a black leather jacket. She'd yodeled her way through her warm-up until her voice was as smooth as her look.

"When everybody is so nervous," LeAnn said, "I can't stand to hear, 'Oh, do this right, do this right.' It's like, 'Let me get out there and do it like I want to and we won't have any problem.' That's what, really, I can't stand."

The members of the audience who awaited LeAnn's big show ranged from some of her former schoolmates to folks old enough to be her grandparents, but they were not the real reason for tonight's performance. The real reason was that Mark Wright was bringing some of his colleagues from Nashville to show them what he'd witnessed back in October.

When only a half hour remained before show time, they still hadn't arrived. This did not help anyone's nerves at all.

But lo and behold, when LeAnn took the stage, there they were at table 14: record producer Mark Wright; Bruce Hinton, chairman of MCA/Nashville; Sheila Shipley, president of Decca Records; and Narvel Blackstock, husband and manager of Reba McEntire.

Before a show actually begins but after performers are dressed, made up, warmed up, and kissed and congratulated by everyone, they have to make that last preparation alone, from the inside. No amount of training can guarantee that they won't fall flat on their face or forget their lines. But right before they go on, they concentrate on the moment of the performance.

Some stars, for example will finish all their meets and greets before the show and then go to what they call a quiet room. It may contain only a chair and some flowers and a bottle of water. Quietly, they sit and collect their thoughts and prepare their energy for the enormous task ahead. Whether they're playing to an intimate room of one hundred or a stadium of one hundred thousand, they have to be ready.

Before LeAnn went out on the stage of the Park Cities Playhouse to make believers out of some of Nashville's most influential record executives, she knew the stakes were high. The flurry of backstage activity around her had been like a hurricane. Questions flew back and forth—How's her hair? Does she look too old? Does she look too young? Does she like the way she looks?

LeAnn was right when she said to just let her get out there and do it. The instinctive, brilliant artist within took over the minute she stepped out on the stage.

The song list and order had already been agreed upon by LeAnn, Wilbur, and the band. The set list requires a lot of deliberation. The performer wants to start out slowly and build up the excitement over the course of the show.

People in the audience may not know the singer. The people at table 14 have seen them all and seen the best. So now they're sitting there saying, as they would say to any new act, Okay, show me what's so great about you. Lots of people can sing; why are you so special?

Once the performer has gotten their attention with one song, they're interested. Then the singer draws them in a little more with the next few in order to hook them. LeAnn had drawn other audiences right into the palm of her hand. She wanted to do it again tonight.

LeAnn sang "I Will Always Love You." Dolly Parton's exquisite song, which Whitney Houston had turned into a megahit, became LeAnn's own for those few minutes.

LeAnn's rockin' country take on Janis Joplin's "Piece of My Heart" showed yet another dimension to her talent.

One song LeAnn had recorded for *All That* brought tears to the eyes of some listeners. "I'll Get Even with

You," written by Coweta House, is about the powerful love and support of a friend who "turned my stumblin' blocks to stepping-stones."

That's the beauty of so many country songs, and maybe it's why more and more people of all ages are finding in country music the kind of characters, story-telling, emotion, and endings—whether happy or sad—that linger with them for a long time after the song is over.

LeAnn sang "Blue." In the Park Cities Playhouse on January 17, 1995, she sang it as beautifully, maybe even with more yearning in her voice, than ever before.

Bill Mack had been so right about that song and that voice. LeAnn Rimes had done even more than Mack had hoped she'd do with his precious song.

In the audience was LeAnn's former teacher, Mrs. Nix. Other members of the audience perked up their ears. LeAnn's classmates—even if they'd heard her sing in the choir—sat up straighter.

It is impossible to hear LeAnn Rimes sing "Blue" and not be moved, amazed, impressed, dazzled, and much, much more.

And it doesn't matter if you've already heard every great singer in the world. It makes no difference that you may have created some of the most thrilling sounds ever to come out of a recording studio. You might have pro-duced some of the most memorable concert tours of the century. Even if you've spent years presiding over major-label record companies and guided the best pros in the business, hearing LeAnn Rimes sing "Blue" is still a sin-gular experience.

How many eyes were nervously staring at table 14? When Narvel Blackstock smiled during one of LeAnn's songs, who gulped? If Mark Wright and Bruce Hinton began whispering to each other as the audience gave LeAnn a standing ovation, what would you think if you'd been working and hoping and praying for her success?

LeAnn put on what she said was the best performance of her career.

The Nashville contingent clapped and smiled and whispered to each other. After the show, a local reporter asked the visiting music executives for their comments. One said they would be keeping their opinions to themselves.

"But their eyes were opened," Rendelman said. "They realized there's too much talent here. Yes, she's a child, we know it's a gamble, but . . ."

Two days later, there was still no word from Nashville. But LeAnn was still giggling at the mere mention of the five standing ovations she had received that cold Tuesday night in January.

"The music business is a tough nut to crack," said Johnnie High. "Sometimes you have to come in the back door, and that may be the case with LeAnn."

LeAnn just waited. In her red, white, and blue bedroom, there were more than four hundred tapes and CDs to listen to, ranging from Faith Hill to Aerosmith to Boyz II Men.

The Garland apartment was getting crowded. "We're hoping to move into a town house," Belinda said, "but right now we're paying month to month until we see what happens. If they do sign LeAnn, we don't know if they'd want us to move.

"We're just playing it by ear."

Decca Records expressed a strong interest in signing LeAnn. Narvel Blackstock reportedly offered to manage her. Other record companies also took LeAnn Rimes very seriously as a potential new act—particularly in the middle of the 1990s. Why? In the late eighties Garth Brooks and Mary Chapin Carpenter brought country music to a whole new audience. Many other acts also sold millions of country CDs, but there were always next year's numbers to consider, and Nashville was always looking for new talent.

LeAnn Rimes Entertainment, Inc., a management company headed by Wilbur Rimes and attorney Lyle Walker, was formed and set up offices in Dallas. LeAnn said they all felt "we would have a little more control of my career if we did it this way."

The Rimeses and Lyle Walker knew LeAnn's talent was like a speeding train: If they didn't get hold of it now, they'd lose all control as it sped down the track.

"The thing we have to do is manage her career very, very carefully," Lyle Walker said. "It would be a shame not to showcase her talents. Her voice is ahead of her age right now and her stage presence is light-years ahead. There's no reason why she can't be a big star."

Known as one of Nashville's more innovative record labels, Curb Records is owned and run by Mike Curb, who was once the lieutenant governor of California.

"Someone sent me her CD," Curb said.

"I was leaving town with my family to drive up to the Great Smoky Mountains. I have two daughters about LeAnn's age. I put it on, and everyone just turned their heads and said, 'Who is that?' We played it all the way up and all the way back, over and over."

Curb had already worked with such teen stars as Marie Osmond and Debby Boone.

"On the way back, I stopped at a pay phone and called her comanager and said, 'We are interested in this artist very much.' "

Curb promised that the Rimeses "could keep control of our daughter," said Wilbur. He would continue to produce LeAnn's music and manage her career.

The announcement in the spring of 1995 that MCG/Curb Records in Nashville had signed LeAnn Rimes to a major recording contract was accompanied by a statement from Dennis Hannon, Curb vice-president and general manager.

"We are thrilled with her incredible talent and anxious to introduce her to country radio," he said. "Nineteen ninety-six will be a very exciting year for us all."

LeAnn had gotten something she'd wanted and worked for all those years. Shortly thereafter, so did her friend and patron, Johnnie High.

In April 1995, he bought an old red-brick theater, complete with a period balcony and an old marquee, on Center Street in Arlington, Texas, and beautifully renovated it. The movie screen was removed and a stage was installed.

After twenty years of moving from one location to another, Johnnie High's Country Music Revue had found a home of its own in the Arlington Music Hall.

CHAPTER FIVE

☆ ☆ ☆

"Blue" Is Red-Hot

Welcome to Billy Bob's Texas in the Fort Worth Stockyards! The world's largest honky-tonk!

With her own entertainment company and a major-label record deal, LeAnn closed 1995 with a huge celebration.

LeAnn's fifth-grade teacher, Mrs. Nix, was in the audience that first night LeAnn appeared at Billy Bob's. "Nothing affected her," Mrs. Nix said. "She just went out and did it."

Wilbur and Belinda had taken LeAnn to a lot of opries and showplaces and concert spots, but Billy Bob's was the ultimate not only for them but for all the top stars of country, who have made it a regular stop on the concert-tour circuit since it opened on April 1, 1981.

No fooling. Billy Bob's has a 100,000-square-foot entertainment center, 40 individual bar stations, and the 1,200-seat Billy Bob's Bull Riding Arena. Yes, they have live bull riding every Friday and Saturday night. The sign says it costs two bucks, and Billy Bob's Texas "History and Fast Facts" insists there's never been a mechanical bull—only 23,000 live ones. There's a pool room, slot and other gaming machines (you win merchandise, not money), and countless neon signs for beer, boots, jeans, hats, and cigarettes. You can shop at Billy Bob's Dry Goods Store, eat at Billy Bob's Texas Bar-B-Q, examine the handprints of famous musicians that line some of the walls, or stop in at the Texas Club, where you might hear a lounge act.

Jim Melton, a bartender at Billy Bob's for about four years, had already seen LeAnn perform. "She was just as good as anyone on that main stage," he said. "Young as she is, her voice is just crisp and clear and you can hear it all over the club." He's talking about a club that covers approximately two and a half acres.

About the only thing you can't do at Billy Bob's, according to signs posted here and there, is dance on the tables.

That was a tough rule to follow on that crisp night in December when LeAnn Rimes, wearing her great Texas boots, belted out her songs and brought down the house.

When Bill Mack learned that LeAnn and Wilbur were cutting a new version of "Blue," he was a little worried. "I didn't think they could improve it. I was afraid they might lose something."

Anything can happen in the recording studio. LeAnn had already sung "Blue" dozens of times onstage both before and after the recording she made of it in the Norman Petty studio in Clovis, New Mexico.

LeAnn had a lot of confidence, and she was already comfortable in the recording studio. But imagine finding yourself at the age of thirteen in Midtown Tone and Volume, a state-of-the-art recording studio in Nashville, Tennessee, the legendary Music City, the very center of the country-music business.

© Acey Harper/People Weekly

© Theo Westenberger

© Paul S. Howell/Gamma Liaison

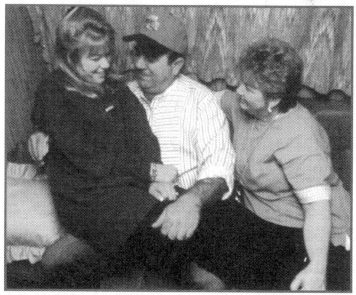

© Acey Harper/People Weekly

© Acey Harper/People Weekly

© John Chiasson/People Weekly

© Steve Granitz/Retna Ltd.

© Acey Harper/People Weekly

© Acey Harper/People Weekly

© John Chiasson/People Weekly

Along with Wilbur, who had been producing her songs since she was two years old, LeAnn was in the presence of top music-business veterans. There were producers, engineers, and musicians, all waiting for her to sing "Blue," one of the songs that had gotten her this far in the first place.

LeAnn cut "Blue," says Wilbur, "using her thirteen-year-old voice instead of her eleven-year-old voice."

Bill Mack was satisfied when he heard it. "They were right," he says. "They put a little more maturity in it at thirteen than she had at eleven."

Making the album that would also be titled *Blue* for MCG/Curb took more than a year. Some of the musical tracks used in the locally released album *All That* were used again. New music was recorded at Rosewood Studio, in Tyler, Texas, and at two studios in Nashville, Midtown Tone and Volume and Omni Sound.

Choosing material for the new album presented something of a challenge. The question for Nashville and the top songwriters who create the music and write the lyrics we come to love was: Who was this thirteen-year-old from Texas with the big voice and big new record deal? Remember, this was before LeAnn was a big star.

To be as generous as possible, she was one lucky girl with a real chance to stand or fall on her own talents. To be realistic, she was another in a long line of talented artists who had gotten that one chance to step up to the plate and hit a home run in the major leagues. More often than not, such people strike out in spite of terrific music and smart marketing. To the cynical—and even in the

polite and congenial atmosphere of Music Row, there's
plenty of skepticism—she was a "novelty act" who
couldn't possibly be expected to have the life experience
to sing about the lovin' and hurtin' and cheatin' and flirtin'
that are the themes of so many country-music songs.

With such thoughts, songwriters and music publishers
were mirroring, perhaps for different reasons, the legiti-
mate concerns Wilbur and Belinda had all along.
Throughout LeAnn's early musical career, they concentrated on their daughter still being a very young girl.
Even her potential for success took a backseat to
LeAnn's development as a person. She was a remarkable young woman and a good human being with a long
life ahead of her that might not always include a career
in the music business. There was little to be gained in
letting her make the wrong moves before she was even
old enough to vote.

When a country superstar is getting ready to make
a record, every veteran and amateur songwriter in
Nashville rushes to "pitch" his or her songs.
Publishers of songs, from small ones with folksy little
names to the big guns such as Sony, EMI, and Warner-
Chappell, send their song pluggers out to meet the
artists and their record producers.

The pluggers play the demo tape and try to convince
the stars that this new song will surely be their next big
hit. There's a lot of money at stake for the songwriter
and publisher when their song is included on a hit
album—and even more if that song becomes a hit single
on the radio.

It was rumored that before Reba made her 1996
album, she had put ninety-three songs on hold—industry

jargon for "I might record this so don't give it to anyone else." With most CDs featuring about ten songs, it's an uphill battle for a songwriter who wants his or her work on an album.

So how do you make a record?

In a club or concert-hall performance, the music—whether magnificent or mediocre—vanishes into the air as soon as it is played. Once it's on the record, it lasts forever, regardless of the quality. Naturally, you want the quality to be excellent.

The studios of Nashville have state-of-the-art equipment and some of the best studio musicians, backup vocalists, record producers, and sound engineers in the business.

All the players have their instruments and their amplifiers in little rooms by themselves to isolate their sounds. They are in eye contact with each other and can hear one another through a headphone monitoring system.

The singer is by herself in a booth with a window so she can see the musicians, most importantly the drummer, who sets the beat of the song.

There's a leader on the session, either one of the musicians or the producer, who will make out charts of the song for each player. The singer will want a chart, too, if she knows about music, and the musicians in Nashville say the good singers know a lot.

The charts allow the people in the studio to communicate with each other during a session. You say, for example, "Let's go back to bar sixteen here and take it from there."

The musicians and the singers already know the song. They begin by playing their instruments and fitting their sounds together. The session leader talks about the song, and the producer gives an overview of the general feel and sound they want to accomplish. Then the band figures out where the guitar solo might go and how the fiddle should fit in and when the steel guitar player will add that distinctive sound.

Slowly, the sound starts to come together. It's a while before they actually go for a full performance of the song. "But you may keep the tape on," says Keith Hinton, one Nashville pro who does it all, from songwriting and singing to playing and producing, "in case magic happens."

Even though a song may be only three minutes and thirty seconds long, the ideal length for radio play—it may take a day or more to record.

We've all heard the words "tracks" or "tracking." That means the song is put together in parts, like an electronic jigsaw puzzle. The singer is there to sing the song, but she often only goes through the motions, just to make a rough blueprint, much like a painter makes a pencil sketch. Sometimes called a "scratch vocal," this vocal track helps the musicians find their individual places and context within the song and record—the bass track, the lead-guitar track, the drum track, and so on.

When all the tracks are done—and there's at least one for each instrument—the singer comes back and really sings it. Now is when she shows off the one instrument that really counts, the one instrument that comes, like LeAnn's does, straight from God, the human voice. This time it's for the record.

All the tracks are then blended together into one seamless song. This is called doing the "mix." It can take hours, sometimes days (and many long nights) to mix one song. If you decide you need some more guitar or a few more vocal flourishes, players and singers come back in to "overdub," which is adding music to what's already on the tracks.

An alternative to creating tracks and putting them together is to try to get the song down in one take. One of the qualities records with the so-called Nashville sound try to convey is the "live" feel of the music. The band and singer perform together as if it were a concert, and record everything all at once.

"There's an old line in Nashville that it takes three minutes to cut a hit record. It's a joke but it's also the truth," Hinton says. "You go in and you just do it. If the musicians communicate well and play well, they go through the whole song at the same time and play it great.

"This gives the singer a wonderful carpet to go out and step out on and then you get magic," said the Nashville pro. "The best records have always been cut that way, at least in my opinion."

Does it happen often? "It is unusual," Hinton continued, "although the best people try to do it. Some singers don't want to record that way. They'd rather wait until the tracks are done. They come back another day and bring the honey and the lemon and the whole deal and they go for it all by themselves and that's fine, too.

"But some of the really good ones, the great singers, they want to go in and just cut it because it's so cool when it happens all at once."

* * *

When she made her first album, *All That,* in New Mexico, LeAnn amazed everyone, especially the veteran studio musicians who were recording with her, by doing so many songs in one take. LeAnn's producer, Wilbur—the perfectionist with perfect pitch—knew whether the one take had nailed the song.

For LeAnn's once-in-a-lifetime-opportunity album for a major Nashville label, Wilbur was under a bit more pressure about recording techniques, song selection, and everything else.

He was more than the album's coproducer. He was the father of the precious creature about to put everything she had out there for all the world to see and hear—and judge.

The folks at MCG/Curb Records in Nashville were unquestionably excited about LeAnn Rimes. Curb is proud of the way that all of its staff pulls together in a team effort and considers that a vital ingredient in its success.

But the combination of excitement and fans inside a record company doesn't always translate to acceptance and sales outside the record company. In fact, when you think of the complicated mix of talent, luck, radio play, good shopping weather, publicity breaks, live appearances, and the countless other elements that come together to make a hit, it seems like a miracle when it happens. And it happens far less frequently than you'd think, given the enormous number of new records that hit the racks and the radio stations all the time.

So the marketing mavens at Curb decided to try a new angle with LeAnn Rimes. Rather than releasing the album first, they opted to put out a single to test the waters via radio. The important programmers who decide what gets played on radio in the first place, as well as the listeners who call up to express their opinions, would have some time to respond to LeAnn Rimes. The company had the album ready to go with a release date several months away. They figured they had some time to make the next move.

Interestingly, the new version of "Blue" wasn't even supposed to be the first single from LeAnn's major album from Curb Records. "The Light in Your Eyes" was slated to fill this role.

Record companies take a number of important steps as they begin to market an artist and her music. One of these is to set up showcases to introduce influential radio programmers to new songs, hoping these powerful execs will respond positively and start broadcasting the song to their listeners.

LeAnn performed at showcases in Nashville at the annual Country Radio Seminar in March 1996. The CRS brings together radio personnel from all over the country to sample the newest "product" from Music City. Like every other big music event that takes place in Nashville, the CRS generates excitement for weeks in advance. Record companies and their marketing departments, public-relations firms, and artists' management offices prepare to meet and greet some of the people who can truly make or break a new song.

MCG/Curb rented a hospitality suite for the occasion, and LeAnn impressed everyone with her poise and maturity. It was a first and important step in gaining the attention—and the respect—of yet another group of music-business veterans who have, literally, heard it all.

LeAnn performed at other showcases, one in Dallas and one at the Gavin Country Seminar in Los Angeles. She also did a showcase in Tampa that was particularly tough.

WXTU Philadelphia program director Kevin O'Neal told *Billboard* about the event.

"They had these risers set up, and I thought, 'They're going to put a thirteen-year-old on there singing to tracks. I don't even want to see the massacre.' " Professional artists singing to tracks is what the rest of us call karaoke. The music comes out of the speakers, and the singer has to sing along with it. It's a difficult way to perform. LeAnn had done it before in her talent shows, and she'd shown herself to be remarkably calm under pressure all her life. Still, even she had to know that these appearances amounted to a make-it-or-break-it moment.

According to O'Neal, "In thirty seconds, we were all spellbound."

To heighten the group excitement record companies hope will be generated at the showcases, special repre-sentatives and promotion experts visit radio stations on behalf of the companies to present the artists and songs to program directors.

Like sales reps in all kinds of industries, these repre-sentatives bring elaborate sales kits featuring key infor-mation about the product and samples to show or play for their customers.

For five months before the release of the album, the folks from MCG/Curb circulated a four-song sample tape and an electronic press kit to radio stations. The kit included the video for "The Light in Your Eyes," still slated to be the first single, and excerpts of four songs: "The Light in Your Eyes," "Hurt Me," "My Baby," and, of course, "Blue."

And everywhere in the sales kit, everywhere in the press releases, everywhere in all the presentations was the sales "hook" that convinced people they had to at least give a listen to this newcomer named LeAnn Rimes.

"She's a thirteen-year-old country singer who sounds like Patsy Cline."

The story of LeAnn Rimes, radio stations, and the song "Blue" is one that begins with excitement and hope, veers into potential heartbreak yet emerges triumphant, though not perfectly so. Just the kind of emotional roller coaster country-music fans love to hear about. And, best of all, it is a story in which country-music fans play a starring role. (Okay, a supporting role—after LeAnn and Bill Mack.)

A lot of the radio programmers who'd heard LeAnn sing "Blue" at the showcases and many who'd heard the song back home during sales presentations at their own radio stations flipped over it and urged MCG/Curb to make it the first single. But quite a few other programmers had doubts. No one could say that LeAnn didn't display amazing vocal skills or that there was anything wrong with the song. And, yes, her singing did evoke the memory of Patsy Cline, although with an unmistakable sound all her own. It's just that the world of country-music radio is not a simple one.

To people outside the music industry, country music

is country music. But that's not so in the world of radio programming, which divides the category into a number of smaller categories. There's traditional country, contemporary country, young country, pop-influenced country, and even subcategories defined in terms of demographics.

For some stations looking to grab the younger audience, "Blue" was just too old-fashioned, with its 1950s style and Patsy Cline connection. In fact, when it was first played in Nashville on radio station WSIX, a number of negative calls came in. Another group of calls was positive.

Clearly, the public was as divided at first in its opinion of this song as was radio. Many radio programmers said they hadn't seen such an intense reaction to a song since Billy Ray Cyrus's "Achy Breaky Heart."

"It's a very odd record," the KSLA Los Angeles program director told *Billboard*. "People say, 'Who is this person, and why is she cracking her voice like that?' It's even produced like an old country song—bare-bones production—so it really sticks out on the radio. But we sure get calls whenever we play it."

Some stations took the plunge and started playing "Blue" as an experiment. They were soon bombarded with requests from fans.

RADIO PROGRAMMERS
IIAVE HEARD IT ALL—
HERE'S WHAT THEY SAY ABOUT LeANN:

Some radio programmers were cautious at first, thinking that the old-fashioned country sound of "Blue" wouldn't satisfy their younger listeners. But they became believers when the fans called in demanding to hear . . . "Blue."

"'Blue' was a phenomenon that you can't apply the rules to. That record had such personality. And it's still continuing. I think it's a safe bet to say that LeAnn Rimes will be a superstar. We had her on as a guest DJ. She was one of the best we've ever had. . . . There's a lot of talent there. The fact that she's thirteen years old is basically irrevelant."

—DENE HALLAM, vice-president of programming, KKBQ-FM, Houston

"LeAnn Rimes is attracting some older folks who don't go out and buy records like the younger people do. She's cut through very quickly in all that noise out there of new artists because of her age, her talent, and 'Blue,' such a different record. But she's absolutely more than a one-hit wonder."

—SMOKEY RIVERS, program director, KPLK-FM, Dallas/*Dallas Morning News*

" 'Blue' has been one of the biggest singles in the last ten years. The question is: Is this the dawn of a career for a new artist or is it just a novelty? I believe, in the end, talent will win out."
—Tony Thomas, KMPS, Seattle, in *USA Weekend*

"You have to be concerned about playing a record that sounds too much like yesterday, but with her youth and freshness this record comes home. I can't think of anybody else who could have sung this song and made it work."
—Kevin O'Neal, WXTU-FM, Philadelphia

"The first time I saw her it just blew me away. I couldn't believe where that voice was coming from. She's going to be a phenomenal act. This is a once-in-a-lifetime kind of performer."
—Ted Cramer, program director, WDAF-AM, Kansas City

"She's . . . got a voice that'll just knock you out. . . . She's gonna go right to the top."
—P. K. Wilde, programmer, KLGAT, Buffalo, Wyoming

"Our phones have absolutely blown off the hook. It's our number one most-requested song."
—Neil McGinley, operations director, WKHX-FM and WYAY-FM, Atlanta

"When we started playing 'Blue' before its official release, instantly people fell in love with it. She's got a tremendous voice and a lot of soul."

—GREG ROCHE, program director,
WWYZ, Waterbury, Connecticut

Program Director Mac Daniels of WMZO, the largest country-music station in the Washington, D.C., area, told the *Washington Post* a great story about "Blue." Daniels gave it to the nighttime DJ, Scott Carpenter, who played the song once and got such an overwhelming response he had to play it three more times.

"It was kids calling, kids' grandparents calling."

The next morning, Gary Murphy, the morning DJ, was getting "a ton of calls." He told Daniels, "We need to play it."

Daniels decided to pull "Blue" from airplay the next day to see if there was any demand. "The hate calls literally rolled in," he says. "People even accused Reba McEntire and Faith Hill of getting to me and paying me so they wouldn't have the competition."

"'Blue' is what we call a 'polarized' record. Because it's such a strong song, there are people who don't like it." That was the assessment of Houston's KKBQ-FM station vice-president of programming, Dene Hallam. But that polarization worked both ways: those who liked it *really* liked it.

* * *

Even before there was a video, which today is a vital tool for breaking a new song, "Blue" debuted at number forty-nine with a bullet on *Billboard*'s Hot Country Singles & Tracks. A bullet on a *Billboard* chart means the song is hot and getting hotter fast. To come on the chart at such a high number—and then to get to number sixteen a mere three weeks later—is very unusual for an unknown singer.

But what isn't unusual about LeAnn Rimes?

"I'm someone who eats, drinks, and sleeps country music," said Wade Jesson, *Billboard*'s country columnist. "This kind of renews your faith that there are some things that can come out of left field. It underscores what Nashville's always been about. And it's welcome reassurance."

Imagine being the father of this little girl. Wilbur had invested everything in his daughter's dreams. If he was having trouble believing that suddenly the dream was coming true, he became convinced on the day he walked into the Texas Land & Cattle Company restaurant in Dallas just as the opening bars of "Blue" came drifting out of the radio.

Wouldn't you be a little choked up? All Wilbur could say was, "I'm just proud."

LeAnn demonstrated once again that she knew a lot about the making of a music career when, on May 15, she spent the entire day calling radio stations to thank them for their support.

And later, when asked by *New Country* magazine what she thought when radio stations didn't unanimously accept "Blue," LeAnn once again showed her smarts.

"I knew to expect it, because it was totally different from what's being played today, the contemporary pop-country radio format, so I don't have any grudge."

Maybe "Blue" was just too different from the lighter, pop-oriented sound called young country. According to Jesson, "It could be that a lot of former pop and rock programmers are not comfortable with traditional records in general."

What did Beverly Smith think when she first heard "Blue" on the radio back in Rankin County, Mississippi?

"You never know because we do have a lot of talented people here, especially in Rankin County. You know, Faith Hill is from Rankin County, right here from Florence," she said. "When [LeAnn's] song came out, we said, Well, her daddy knew what he was talking about. I always thought she was good but didn't really think anything more about her being a star at fourteen.

"I thought it was just local stations playing it at first and then I had people asking me about her, and I said, 'Oh, that little hotshot made it.' "

The phone calls kept pouring in and fans told radio: We love "Blue" and we want you to play it. One record store called radio station WXTU in Philadelphia ten minutes after they played the song for the first time because a customer wanted to buy it. There's even the story that in one city, the telephone company asked disc jockeys to stop playing the song for a while because callers were overloading the lines with requests for it. Fans' requests to radio stations made "Blue" one of the fastest rising singles in pop-music history.

* * *

And those same fans who voted with phone calls to their local radio stations marched into record stores looking to buy the record. There was just one problem: no record to buy. Even the record company was surprised by how fast "Blue" was catching on. But MCG/Curb moved quickly to meet the demand. The single on cassette and CD hit the record racks in stores across the country on June 4. And, as is customary, a good old-fashioned 45 record was specifically made for jukebox operators.

The first day in stores, fans bought more than one hundred thousand copies of the single.

"I'm overwhelmed more than anything," LeAnn said. "I just can't believe this is happening, especially with my first single. When I heard that it had debuted at number forty-nine in *Billboard,* I was just like, 'Oh my gosh!' "

"We're talking about a first week that new artists dream of, but only superstars have," said Steve Lee, Curb promotion director for the Southwest region.

A video wasn't made for "Blue" at first because no one was prepared for the speed of its popularity. But this deficiency was quickly remedied as a video was put together for Country Music Television (CMT) and the Nashville Network (TNN). The video was taped at the recording studio and in Zilker Park in Texas.

Austin's Barton Springs in Zilker Park is famous for its botanical gardens and nature preserve, where three million gallons of water from the underground Edwards aquifer bubble up every day. Native Americans who settled near this natural spring-fed pool believed the waters had spiritual powers. Today, people find the 1,000-by-125-foot pool very soothing, with its year-round temperature of sixty-eight degrees.

In the video for "Blue," LeAnn sings the song with complete seriousness and looks every bit the professional artist inside a recording studio. That version is intercut with takes of LeAnn floating around in the Barton Springs pool, wearing cat-eye sunglasses, enjoying herself immensely as she belts out her song, looking older than her thirteen years.

The video for "Blue" is played very frequently on Country Music Television. Indeed, LeAnn's granddaddy, Thad Butler, said, "Every morning I get up and turn on the TV before I go to work. I see the video; it's on around every hour."

During a visit with Mr. Butler at his home in Pearl, it was heartwarming nearly to the point of tears to sit in silence and watch him watch LeAnn in the "Blue" video. What family member, particularly the proudest one of all, a grandparent, wouldn't be thrilled to see a loved one sing her breakthrough hit on a wonderful video?

And even though radio didn't unanimously embrace "Blue," record buyers did. It had an unprecedented twenty-week run at the top of the *Billboard* Top Country Singles sales chart.

Now everyone in Nashville was talking about "that girl" singing "that song"—fans in their teens and twenties who hadn't even heard of Patsy Cline, baby boomers with kids LeAnn's age, and grandparents who'd listened to and loved Patsy Cline for years. They all agreed in the early summer of 1996 that this was something special in the world of country music.

There aren't any actual reports of people driving off the road when their car radios entranced them with the starkly simple yet instantly gripping sound of LeAnn singing "Blue." But one fan told LeAnn he had to pull onto the side of the road the first time he heard it because it gave him goose bumps. Many a volume button was turned up and many a soul, young and old, felt in LeAnn's plaintive rendition the true emotion Bill Mack had written into the song.

"I've never sat up at three in the morning wondering if a guy is going to come home," LeAnn says. We believe you, honey, but you'd never know it from that performance.

"I think we knew it was a good song, but I didn't know it would be this big a hit," LeAnn said from a tour stop in Seattle. "This has been really fun for my whole family."

There was another reason radio programmers came to love "Blue." Television has the Nielsen ratings to measure the popularity of TV programs. In the sweeps months of November and February those ratings are very important in helping the stations determine their advertising rates. (That's why TV is often so good in those months.) Well, radio stations have their Arbitron ratings, which work the same way as the Nielsens. Across America, radio stations were delighted to have a song people were talking about during the critical spring ratings period.

Nashville was particularly happy to have a ray of sunshine in the form of an exciting new artist with a big hit in the middle of 1996. The country-music business had grown to huge proportions, selling millions and millions of records each year since Garth Brooks and others had brought country music out of Oklahoma, Texas, and Nashville and all the way to both coasts in the late eighties. Other artists had also racked up impressive sales.

But in mid-'96, record company executives and music retailers were experiencing a collective headache over the decline in sales. Now, it wasn't that sales were bad, they were just lower than they had been.

So Nashville needed some good news to cure the uneasiness on Music Row.

Music Row in Nashville consists of several long avenues and streets filled with record companies, artists' management offices, music-publishing companies, recording studios, public-relations firms, cassette and CD duplicating services, and all the other large and small businesses that support the music industry. In a way, it's like a college town, even including some very popular restaurants and bars. A music-biz pro can barely walk down the street without running into a colleague and maybe starting a deal on the spot.

Many of these businesses are housed in sleek, low-rise office buildings. BMI, ASCAP, and SESAC, the major companies that monitor radio airplay and see that artists and writers get their royalties, have particularly dramatic-looking and beautiful buildings. But most businesses have their offices in what were formerly residential houses, many built during the Arts and Crafts era, with big front porches, gorgeous entryways that serve now as reception rooms, and large offices in the

living rooms, dining rooms, and bedrooms. These set-
tings create a casual and friendly atmosphere for listening to music, tossing around ideas, and working with a
lot of team spirit.

When LeAnn first got her Curb Records deal, there
was, as always, a "buzz" about it up and down the row.
Throughout the spring of 1996, people were talking. A
thirteen-year-old country singer from Texas? A major
deal at such an early age? Who was this girl? At first, for
many people, it simply didn't compute.

"I think Nashville's been kind of skeptical about
young singers," LeAnn said, "but when Mike Curb
called us last year and wanted to do something, there
were more young people getting into the business like
Bryan White and Mandy Barnett, and that helped a lot."

By June, LeAnn Rimes and "Blue" were *great* news.
What made things even sweeter for LeAnn and better
for Nashville was that her big break was happening just
as Music City was getting ready for Fan Fair.

No other sector of the entertainment business does
for its fans what country music does.

The International Country Music Fair, cosponsored
by the Country Music Association (the first trade organization formed to promote, nationally and interna-
tionally, any type of music) and the Grand Ole Opry
(country's most beloved and important stage), is a
huge festival that brings artists and their fans together
for a weeklong lovefest. The main events are held at
the Tennessee State Fairgrounds in Nashville. At other
locations all over town, artists host special events for

fan club members. Everyone holds parties.

The first Fan Fair, held in April 1972 at Nashville's Municipal Auditorium, was attended by five thousand people. The next year, it was moved from April to June, a peak travel month with better weather, and attendance doubled. The third Fan Fair was highlighted by an appearance by ex-Beatle and country-music fan Paul McCartney, and the last performance together of the beloved country duo Porter Wagoner and Dolly Parton.

In 1996, Fan Fair celebrated its twenty-fifth anniversary with a full-tilt-boogie blowout. As in the previous six years, it was sold out months in advance, with attendance capped at twenty-four thousand fans. These fans from all over the world, along with two hundred artists and one hundred booths, countless publicists, record-company people, managers, and booking agents, would fill the fairground to its maximum capacity.

Each attendee bought a ninety-dollar ticket that included all the fairground events as well as admission to the Ryman Auditorium (the former home of the Grand Ole Opry), the Country Music Hall of Fame (a museum with rare and wonderful country-music artifacts and memorabilia), and Opryland USA (the new home of the Opry as well as other theaters and attractions, a mega-amusement park, and an out-of-this-world hotel). Also included were two free lunches served up by the Odessa Chuck Wagon Gang of Odessa, Texas: a Texas menu of barbecue, beans, slaw, onions, pickles, bread, and beverages.

Established artists at the top of the field always make time for Fan Fair—and they don't get paid. "These artists come off the road for a full week in midseason to sit at tables for eight or ten hours," said Dennis Hannon, executive vice-president of Curb Records. "It's a way to pay back fans for their support."

Fan Fair 1996 took place amid the usual mix of dense humidity, thunderstorms, and searing sunshine that characterize Nashville summers. But weather never stopped the party. The big record labels held daily concerts at the Nashville Motor Speedway. A thrilling line-up of stars performed on the huge stage on a pretty tight schedule while their fans were given the chance to file by in a single line to get a closer look and, if they were lucky, snap a photograph.

On Tuesday, Curb Records' day for the stage, a light rain was falling, which cooled the temperature a bit. The audience was a mix of wide-eyed fans, music-business insiders, and many of the more than six hundred media representatives from such countries as Switzerland, Japan, Brazil, Sweden, Spain, England, Ireland, Luxembourg, and France. Onstage was "new artist" LeAnn Rimes.

"Blue," and all the Patsy Cline and Brenda Lee comparisons it occasioned, had created the demand. Now all eyes and ears were on LeAnn at Fan Fair. Someone commented that it looked like a scene out of *A Star Is Born* right there on the Curb stage.

LeAnn took to the stage, lifted the microphone, and, as she'd done hundreds of times before, put on a top-notch performance, complete with the yodels, gasps, and torchy country/blues phrasing that had already captivated so many listeners.

How wonderful that the number one country single on the sales chart that week was "Blue." When LeAnn sang it, this newcomer to Music City proved she knew traditional country. After "Blue," LeAnn switched gears. "This is my favorite song on the record," she announced, and launched into "One Way Ticket (Because I Can)."

The crowd gave her a standing ovation.

Back at her bus after the show, LeAnn and her parents were surrounded by fans and journalists and camera crews from near and far. As a camera crew from the Netherlands took its turn looking inside the Rimes tour bus, Wilbur, wearing a red polo shirt emblazoned with the words LEANN RIMES ENTERTAINMENT, INC., shook his head. "I still can't quite believe it," he said.

As network camera crews buzzed around, Belinda said, "I'm just amazed, absolutely amazed, and a nervous wreck."

"I'm happy for her," said Nashville songwriter Wayne Perry, "but I hope she's careful. I've seen this so many times. I call it Fame and Misfortune. An artist works so hard to get to the top of the mountain, but things look really different once you're up there. I hope there's someone there to protect her."

In one day at Fan Fair, LeAnn had instantly made believers out of people who'd hardly known who she was a few months—actually, a few weeks!— earlier.

Top Nashville anchorwoman Demetria Kalodimos praised LeAnn and called her an overnight sensation. "Not really," LeAnn replied with that amazing poise and grace. "I've been doing this for eight years."

Fan Fair continued for the rest of the week, with fans enjoying great performances, shopping for T-shirts, buttons, and banners, and carefully planning their time to get as many autographs and pictures as possible. Many of these folks became friends while they waited and will meet again at Fan Fair next year. Their worship of the stars creates a special bond, as does the courteous and hospitable atmosphere of Nashville, one of the friendliest cities on earth.

The rest of the summer of 1996, "Blue" was the number one single in sales, though it only reached number ten on radio. A few big country stations still wouldn't play it because they felt its old-fashioned sound didn't fit their newer formats. But LeAnn continued to make fans of people from ten to a hundred years old. Suddenly, this amazing young star, who seemed to people to be a genuinely real, sweet person, was everyone's daughter, granddaughter, and friend.

As for Bill Mack, he was the happiest man in show business after LeAnn turned "Blue" into the huge hit he had imagined it would be for Patsy Cline decades earlier.

"Everybody is saying the same thing, that she's another Patsy Cline," Mack told the *Dallas Morning News*. "In the styling, yes, there's a similarity. She also has the same thing Ray Charles has—soul. She sings from the heart. You can tell that when you watch her onstage."

CHAPTER SIX

☆ ☆ ☆

Dream Come True

"One thing I'm not is shy," LeAnn said. "It's hard to be shy and make it in this business."

July 9, 1996, was the "street date" for *Blue*. Tractor trailers covered with pictures of LeAnn's album had traveled all over the country delivering CDs and cassettes to every imaginable kind of store where music is sold. This was the moment of truth for LeAnn, and for Wilbur and Belinda Rimes, too. All the people involved in LeAnn's career—her band, comanager Lyle Walker, the entire Curb record- company staff involved in the launch of the album—were holding their breath.

The high-powered Rogers & Cowan public-relations firm in Los Angeles had already pumped the media full of stories about the phenomenal success of the single. "Thirteen-year-old country singer" was how most of America knew LeAnn Rimes, even if they hadn't heard her name or her song. Creative Artists Agency's Nashville headquarters was booking LeAnn into the busy summer concert circuit on important indoor and outdoor stages as the opening act for some of the biggest names in country music.

All over the music business and all over the country, the expectations for LeAnn's first major album were huge.

If she hadn't made such a splash with the song "Blue," she wouldn't have had such a high note to beat. On the other hand, she wouldn't have aroused the interest and curiosity of so many people in the first place. So the pressure was on LeAnn, and though she didn't show it, she had to be a little worried and very, very excited.

In the final selection of songs for *Blue*, LeAnn, who has a big say in the choice of material, revealed another streak of brilliance. Not only did the songs showcase her spectacular voice and amazing five-to-six-octave range but none seemed inappropriate for her age.

"I might not have lived it yet," she says in response to the oft-asked question, "but I know what it's about, so I can basically feel the song. I don't think I have to live it to sing it."

Wilbur adds his own spin to the subject. "Once she gets her heart broke, look out."

Of course, the first song was "Blue."

"Hurt Me," written by Deborah Allen, Rafe Van Hoy, and Bobby Braddock, is sung by LeAnn with the same heartfelt pain that made "Blue" so believable. The wise sentiment of "Honestly," by Christi Dannemiller and Joe Johnston, that it's better to be left kindly than loved insincerely, is pure musical magic in LeAnn's interpretation. LeAnn brings true grace and spirit to Dan Tyler's "The Light in Your Eyes" and to Coweta House's "I'll Get Even with You," which she'd recorded previously on *All That*.

"My Baby," by Deborah Allen, and Joyce Harrison's

"Good Lookin' Man" show that LeAnn has what it takes to ratchet up the rhythm. In "Talk to Me," which LeAnn wrote along with Ron Grimes and Jon Rutherford, she sets her sweet voice rocking. "I'm really excited about "Talk to Me,' and I'm looking forward to continuing my songwriting," she said.

"Cattle Call" is a duet that LeAnn sings with Eddy Arnold. Arnold, now in his eighties, continues a half century of touring the country singing and playing his music. "At first, I was his granddaughter, and then I graduated to his daughter," LeAnn says, smiling. "He is a very, very nice guy." According to LeAnn, it was "an honor to sing with such a great man and living legend."

Finally, there's the song that may have been the last chosen for the album but would become another first for LeAnn. "One Way Ticket (Because I Can)" was written by Judy Rodman and Keith Hinton. LeAnn sings it with all the triumph and celebration of a young woman in charge of her own destiny.

The song "Unchained Melody," which has been around for decades, was a Righteous Brothers hit, and found more fame as the song from the hit movie *Ghost*, was recorded for *Blue* but not included on the final album.

"There's not been a day that's gone by for the past month that I haven't been doing something," LeAnn said early last summer. And the big touring season was about to begin.

LeAnn kicked off her first bus tour at Billy Bob's on June 22. She was returning in triumph for her first show there since "Blue" had blown to the top of the singles chart, and now drew more than three thousand people.

"We have a lot of young artists that even with a top-ten or number one record or two have not put those kind of numbers in the building," said Robert Gallagher, entertainment coordinator for Billy Bob's.

"Obviously one of the hooks is that she's thirteen years old; that in itself is unusual," Gallagher continued. "Once they hear the voice, perfect pitch, and she can really deliver a live performance, they are just aston-ished. There's all kinds of hooks to get them to listen, and once they listen, she delivers."

Johnnie High agrees. "I see these young acts, and they haven't been working a lot. But she has. It's hard to beat getting on a stage every week. She's only thirteen, but she's a tough girl and she knows what she wants."

On July 7, in the showroom of Van Zandt Realtors at the Ballpark in Arlington, Texas, more than two hundred people gathered to celebrate the release of LeAnn Rimes's first major-label album. Johnnie and Wanda High were there. The Rimes family came in from Mississippi for the big occasion. Local media, along with radio reporters and a television crew from Jackson, recorded the big event.

The Ballpark had been open only a couple of months. The magnificent baseball-only facility is the centerpiece of a 270-acre complex that includes a baseball museum, an office building, facilities for children and teens, two lakes, and other recreational facilities. The open-air sta-dium seats almost fifty thousand fans. The granite-and-brick facade, and the Texas architecture throughout the facility, is stunningly beautiful.

Jamie Adams, a Van Zandt real-estate agent, organizes many events throughout the greater Dallas area. An expert in personal management and promotional events, she's also credited with handling home sales for some of the members of the Texas Rangers. For this occasion, she had created another sensational party.

The room was buzzing and thumping with congratulations, hugs, kisses, and slaps on the back. There wasn't a doubt in that room that the album *Blue* would be as successful as the song. These were LeAnn's original fans, her hometown cheerleaders, and they were delighted to see their local sweetheart make it into the big time. Wilbur and Belinda beamed all night. Looks like they'd been right about their daughter all along.

Blue debuted at number one on the *Billboard* country-music charts. It bumped Shania Twain's album, *The Woman in Me*, which had been the biggest country record of the year and a phenomenon in its own right, from the top of the charts. Everyone in the business called *Blue* the biggest debut ever by a new country star. And SoundScan, which monitors cash-register sales of records, confirmed that it was the biggest debut since they had begun tabulating in May 1991.

But that wasn't all. *Blue* also came in at number three on the pop-music charts, meaning it wasn't just country fans who were waking up to the fresh new sound of LeAnn Rimes.

LeAnn was on tour in Kansas City when she heard the news.

"It's really cool, I still can't believe it's happening," she said. "I can't get over this. I never expected it. They kept telling me, 'It's going to do this' and 'It's going to do that,' but I never thought it actually would."

Even though "Blue" the single never made it higher than number ten, and the second single from the album, "Hurt Me," didn't get past number forty, the album remained at the top of the charts all summer and well into the fall.

Asked if people in Pearl talk to him about LeAnn, Thad Butler smiled, nodded, and said, "They all know I'm her granddaddy."

"Seeing your daughter get the career she's wanted since she was five years old," Wilbur said, "is the best feeling ever."

About her parents, LeAnn said, "I think I've pushed them more than they've ever tried to push me. I'm very grateful for them helping me out."

Belinda "never thought it would get this big."

The only one who wasn't surprised was LeAnn. "Deep down, I always knew it would happen," she said. "It's just happening a lot faster than I ever dreamed."

That same conviction propelled Celine Dion, another of LeAnn's musical idols, to the top. The French Canadian superstar, another of the great voices of our time, told ABC's Joan Lunden on the show *Behind Closed Doors* that she started performing professionally at twelve years old and that all her life, she knew she would be a star.

That unshakable inner belief and determination is as important a factor as talent and opportunity in hitting it big at any age. Perhaps being a child adds another vital dimension: Their innocence and wide-eyed wonder at the world isn't yet clouded by disappointment or cynicism. The sun comes out every day, doesn't it? Storybooks have happy endings. In the mind of children such as LeAnn, there's no reason your dream can't come true.

All areas of music have spawned amazing child stars. In the 1950s, Frankie Lymon, a teenage tenor, made "Why Do Fools Fall in Love?" a doo-wop classic. A young rocker named Joan Jett played a mean guitar in the 1970s. Marie Osmond hit the pop and country charts at the age of fourteen, and the young Osmond Brothers went on to have a series of hits. King of Pop Michael Jackson was six when the Jackson 5 first inspired baby boomers to sing along to their rhythm-and-blues classics.

Two of the most enduring and successful child prodigies are Brenda Lee and Stevie Wonder. Both began recording at the age of eleven. Brenda Lee began recording in Nashville in 1956 with Owen Bradley, who had produced Patsy Cline. She toured with fifties rock-and-roll trailblazers Carl Perkins and Chuck Berry and is remembered for songs ranging from the rockabilly "Rockin' Around the Christmas Tree" to the ballad "I'm Sorry."

CHEERS FROM BRENDA LEE

"I guess it's natural that I would root for LeAnn's career, as we are so often compared for starting out so young with hits. I loved her style and presentation, from the first time I was driving along and heard 'Blue' on the radio! Needless to say, I turned it up. . . . Now, having worked with her onstage, I have respect for her not only as a singer but as a young woman with a clear direction for her life—I think she'll be a great addition to the music industry for years to come."

—Brenda Lee

Any talk about starting out young always includes Brenda Lee. When she was three, in 1947, she could sing a song after hearing it only twice. She won a trophy for singing "Take Me Out to the Ball Game" when she was five, and by the age of seven she had a regular spot on an Atlanta radio show. Soon she was a TV regular, on everything from Atlanta's local program *TV Ranch* to *The Ed Sullivan Show*.

She signed with Decca Records in 1956 and cut "Rockin' Around the Christmas Tree." She had her first number one hit with the ballad "I'm Sorry" and went on to have countless other pop and country hits. When she went to England in the early 1960s as a rock artist, her opening act was the Beatles.

In a career that continues today with touring and traveling the world over, Brenda Lee is an international star. This musical giant is only four feet, eleven inches tall. Her nickname is Little Miss Dynamite.

Little Stevie Wonder, as he was first called, came
from Michigan. Although blind from birth, he could
play numerous musical instruments at an early age.
His singing and songwriting skills have made him one of
the most admired superstars of our time.

LeAnn was also making history, and she didn't even
fit into any particular musical category or style of the
moment. In her case, true talent was the engine that propelled such a stunning rise.

When asked by *Music Row* magazine if Curb
Records had foreseen this huge success, Chuck Howard
laughed.

"Not a chance," he said. "You think we'd sign a girl
who yodels if we were chasing trends all the time? If
there's a company philosophy, it's that you make the
best record an artist is capable of making, and then you
sell it wherever and however you can."

Dozens of songs come out of hundreds of country
radio stations across the country all the time. People in the
music business will tell you a hard fact of life: Just
because people love to hear certain songs and certain
artists on the radio doesn't mean they'll actually go out to
buy a CD or cassette. Those ten or fifteen dollars could be
spent on all kinds of other entertainment or at the grocery
store, at the gas station, or to pay the baby-sitter. So when
fans vote with their dollars, you know they really *love*
what they're hearing.

"This shows you that people want great singers and
great songs and don't care about formats or age," said

Chuck Howard to the *Dallas Morning News.* "Yes, she's thirteen and it gets a lot of press, it's a lot for people to talk about. But she's a great singer. I wouldn't care if she's a hundred. She will be around for a long time."

"First, people ask me if they can see my driver's license," LeAnn said. "It's like, I don't have one, I couldn't get one. Then they say, 'Can we see your birth certificate?' 'Well,' I go, 'I don't have it on me.'

"I don't really wish I was older," she said. "I mean, I do because all my friends are so much older than me, but I have to live with who I am. I don't mind it at all being thirteen. I'll grow up soon enough. I really will!"

The album placed on the *Billboard* 200 chart, a ranking of all albums in all musical categories. It went as high as number three in 1996.

Critics and reviewers praised LeAnn and her album.

One prestigious reviewer, Richard Corliss, had this to say about LeAnn in *Time* magazine: "Rimes has taken that popcorn-kernel-in-the-throat catch, married it to old-fashioned yodeling, and become a crossover star. Her voice breaks with startling ease and, in a microsecond, pole-vaults from barroom belter in the low register to choir girl in the high."

Now, to be fair, not everybody fell in love with everything about LeAnn or her album. Some commented that too many songs required a level of experience beyond her years. Some said she still needed room to grow. Others thought the high-tech and polished sound of Nashville was at odds with the spontaneous and youthful exuberance of LeAnn's singing style.

* * *

"She's got a little bit of a lot of people in her voice," said Patsy Cline's widower, Nashville veteran Charlie Dick. "I hear Brenda Lee. I hear Patsy. I hear other people."

Most fans hear only LeAnn. There's no question that she's spent her young life doing her homework and listening to, and learning from, the great singers who came before her. When someone is smart enough and determined enough and confident enough at age five to declare to her family that she's going to be a professional singer and a star, she's obviously got more than talent. She's got the wisdom to know she can take nothing for granted, that preparation is the key to accomplishing anything great, and that the old joke—"How do you get to the Grand Ole Opry?" "Practice, practice, practice"—isn't really a joke at all.

So Charlie Dick is right. Listening to Barbra Streisand, Celine Dion, and Judy Garland gave LeAnn one version of the female voice and its possibilities. Studying Dolly Parton, Reba McEntire, Trisha Yearwood, and Wynonna filled in another part of her musical education. And it surely helped to be coached and encouraged by Wilbur Rimes from virtually the beginning of her life.

But it's the comparison to Patsy Cline that keeps getting repeated.

All those comparisons to Patsy Cline were the hook that got LeAnn listened to in the first place. Robert K. Oermann is a well-known music critic and journalist based in Nashville. He told CBS's *48 Hours*, "Patsy Cline is unquestionably the shadow that hangs over all female country performers. She was the ultimate." But he continued, "LeAnn Rimes is world-class all the way. Definitely from the heart, à la Patsy."

For LeAnn, "It's a big honor to be compared with such a great singer. . . . When she sang, she felt the music. She made you live it. And a lot of people tell me even though I haven't, I make them feel like that I have."

LeAnn told many people who asked her about all the Patsy Cline comparisons, "It's neat to be compared to her. She's the first person I ever really listened to singing. She's definitely one of my idols. But I also want people to know I can sing other things besides Patsy Cline stuff. I want everyone to know me for me.

"I love the traditional country," LeAnn said, "but I also like the contemporary country."

And, as for her age, LeAnn has repeatedly tried to downplay that as a "hook" or a reason to listen to her. She keeps referring people to her music and continually asks to be judged on her singing and not be regarded merely as this year's novelty.

She told the *Los Angeles Times*: "There is a novelty part to it, but I want to be known as an artist, not as just a thirteen-year-old person that can kind of sing. I want to be known as an artist just like Reba and Wynonna are known as artists."

Does she set high standards for herself? Yes. She always has. But time and again she lives up to them, and we have every reason to believe she will continue to push herself to achieve everything she wants.

"It definitely has helped me being a 'thirteen-year-old singing sensation,'" LeAnn said. "But I want people to know me for my music. Not for my age, because the age is going to go away. I won't be thirteen forever."

The whirlwind of success—true, measurable, undeniable success—continued throughout the summer of 1996. No matter what else ever happens in her life, for LeAnn Rimes, that summer will be one to remember and savor her whole life. Johnnie High was bursting with pride. "You know, this success has not changed her one iota. She still calls me 'Mister Johnnie' in that sweet little Southern-girl voice."

Newspapers from coast to coast wrote about her. Every local and national TV show wanted her. In the Dallas offices of LeAnn Rimes Entertainment, Inc., the phone rang constantly, while out on the road, LeAnn and her entourage kept rolling into city after city, town after town, show after show. Her parents accompanied her to every performance.

Her tour bus was home, office, dressing room, schoolroom, and the place to just relax when a few moments could be found. To all the media, LeAnn repeated the story of her life and continued to demonstrate the amazing poise that kept blowing the minds of everyone who met her. "She's only thirteen," they kept reporting. Thirteen and she's a huge star.

How did all this affect her personally? How in the world did Wilbur and Belinda deal with the endless rush of people to see and places to go and phone calls to return and plans to make? How would any family deal with it? In numerous interviews, the Rimeses kept answering these questions again and again.

"My job right now," Belinda Rimes said, "is to keep her head on straight, keep her honorable."

According to Wilbur Rimes, "She's proud of what she's done. But it's not a spoiled kind of proud."

How easy it would have been for LeAnn to get caught up in the crazy world her beautiful voice had summoned into existence around her. But in the midst of all the hoopla, she kept her smarts.

"It's been a dream of mine forever," she said. "I've been doing this for eight years now, so it doesn't seem that quick to me. It's been a long road."

Did she consider herself a superstar? "I've seen so many people get kind of a big head and think they're better than everybody else," she said. "I don't think I'm better than anyone who's buying a ticket. Everybody has a different talent. A lot of people out there have talents that I don't. So as long as I keep that thought, I think I'll be okay and not get that big-head kind of thing."

But as every musician who's ever spent weeks away from home will tell you, life on the road isn't all parties and applause. It's a hectic time of traveling, sleeping when you can fit it in, doing sound checks, talking to reporters, trying to call home, doing your laundry, and more—all while living on a bus or running from airport to taxi to hotel room to concert stage.

"People think traveling is glamorous," LeAnn said, "which it can be, but part of it isn't glamorous at all. But when you get where you're going and do the show, that's what it's all about."

"Seeing all my fans and how they react to my music is pretty neat," she said. "But I'm never really home anymore and that's hard. I have pictures of my family in my

bunk, and they make it easier to be away so much."
LeAnn's home schooling continues to be an important part of her daily routine. "I have a tutor who travels with me on the bus, and we have to find time for schoolwork in between all the other stuff," she said. "You've got to try to balance it all," Belinda Rimes said. "There's a lot for all of us to learn."

"It's just a lot of fun," LeAnn says. "The best part is going out onstage and seeing the fans, how they like your music and singing along with you. It's really neat."

The amazing impact LeAnn Rimes has had on the country-music business may at first seem overstated. But consider this assessment from veteran music-business journalist Chet Flippo in an article for *Billboard* entitled "The State of the Country: After the Gold Rush":

> On almost every front the gold (and platinum) rush is over. Only one front has not leveled off, and that's a front where the public has voted with its pocketbook. That's the LeAnn Rimes front, where this unheralded thirteen-year-old popped up with a decades-old retro song. . . .

Flippo pointed out that for a long time many in the business felt too many artists sounded the same. The public's demand for radio airplay of "Blue," and the reported stampede into record stores that followed, showed that listeners could still make the difference in bringing music they liked to the forefront of the business.

"It really does catch people's attention because it's

really different from what country music is all about right
now," LeAnn said. "A lot of today's country music is pop
country and the new contemporary stuff. On my album,
we have the new contemporary stuff and also the traditional stuff. I think 'Blue' is just so different from what is
being played on the radio."

LeAnn spent most of August on the road. On Friday,
August 2, she made her first visit to Chicago, opening
for seasoned star Sammy Kershaw at Star Plaza Theater
in Merrillville. Thirteen concert dates, plus interviews
and personal appearances, took her from Merrillville
southwest to San Diego, up north to Vancouver, and
back east in a lopsided circle to Indiana again, this time
in Noblesville.

"One of the biggest worries I have is traveling from
climate to climate and keeping LeAnn well," Belinda
said. "I'm sure it's the same for every entertainer."

Traveling with her mom and dad, six band members,
her comanager, her soundman, and her tutor, LeAnn was
enjoying herself immensely. Those gymnastics classes
she took to give her stamina onstage were sure paying
off. Entertaining a different audience almost every night
and giving them a show they'll remember forever is
exhausting even for stars accustomed to the demands of
the road. Wilbur was glad LeAnn was up to the task.
"Performing at Johnnie High's," he said, "gave her the
stage performance skills she's now using on the road."

THE BAND ON THE BUS

"I've known them since I was six or
seven, so they're like brothers and sisters,"
LeAnn said. "Most of my friends are the
band."

Blue Country, LeAnn's backup band,
features many veteran Dallas-area studio
musicians. On the bus, when she's not
studying with her tutor, she loves to hang
out with her backup.

"We either work out or play games or
watch movies. That kind of stuff," she
says. "This is so much fun, I wouldn't
trade it for anything."

THE BAND'S-EYE VIEW OF LeANN

"She's scary—in a good way. Traveling with
her I get to see the thirteen-year-old. But
when it comes to music, she knows what
she wants. She's savvy."
—**Fred Gleber**, drummer

"I've been in the music business for more than thirty years. The good Lord blessed this little lady with so much talent. Her cup runneth over."
—**Junior Knight**, steel guitarist

"When I heard her sing, her age didn't matter. . . . We're the only band with a curfew."
—**Curtis Randall**, bass player

Kevin Bailey plays acoustic guitar and harmonica and also sings harmony. He left his position in Johnnie High's house band to become LeAnn's bandleader and backup singer.

Johnnie High encouraged him to go even though Bailey was also the building manager. "It was a pretty good loss for me," High said, "but they needed him." Blue Country also features **Jerry Methany** on lead guitar and **Kelly Glenn** on keyboard and harmony vocals.

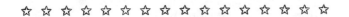

LeAnn opened for another phenomenal musician, Dwight Yoakam, at the Blockbuster Desert Sky Pavilion in Phoenix, Arizona, on Sunday, August 11. She left the crowd in a frenzy.

Yoakam, whose incredible mix of country and rock has made him popular with both audiences, also knew from an early age that he wanted to be a musician. He started writing country songs when he was eight. From the stages of Nashville, where he satisfied traditional country fans, to the honky-tonks of California's San Fernando Valley, where his great mix of rock and country wins him praises, Yoakam is a singular presence in music—and now even in movies, following his highly praised performance in *Sling Blade*.

Though her stardom was evident to anyone who hadn't been living in a soundproof booth wearing a blindfold all summer, LeAnn hadn't worked so hard for so long to take anything for granted.

"I'm very involved in the business part of my career," she said. "That's one thing I don't stay out of. . . . I want to know what's going on. Because it's my life."

At the height of her summer of success, one of the supermarket tabloids ran a story speculating that maybe LeAnn Rimes wasn't really thirteen and that the age thing was just a gimmick invented to push a career. Of course that's not true. Still, some of LeAnn's comments to the press do show a maturity that is remarkable at any age.

"If I had to model my career after anyone, it would be Reba," she said. "She's made some great business decisions in her career to stay around for twenty years, and my biggest goal right now is to stay around for a long time."

LeAnn had all the energy she needed to keep on keeping on. But what about her parents? While they're only in their forties, any forty-something will tell you they don't have the same stamina they did at fourteen.

Belinda Rimes revealed one strategy for dealing with the merry-go-round. "Some of the time, when I really feel tired and I'm thinking, 'Whew! Can I go on from here?' [LeAnn] gets on that stage and the people start going crazy and you think, 'She's having a good time.' What can you do? She's enjoying every minute of it. You'd be behind her one hundred percent."

Wilbur expressed the concern common to every parent of a young star. "How do you let her be a child? You just about can't do that."

Almost everyone in Nashville (and you don't have to be in the music business to get caught up in the excitement) begins biting their fingernails and tossing and turning in the weeks before the Country Music Association announces the nominations for their prestigious awards. It's the country-music equivalent of an Oscar or an Emmy, the most highly coveted trophy in a town and an industry with more than their share of awards.

The CMA Awards, inaugurated in 1967, are presented annually in twelve categories to outstanding country artists, as voted by CMA's membership, to honor excellence in artistry. Every year since 1969, the gala event has been broadcast live over network television.

For performers in any field of entertainment, public acceptance is obviously important to one's career. If you're a musician, that acceptance comes in the form of requests to have your songs played on the radio. The sales of your CDs are incredibly rewarding. If the public doesn't want to hear the music you're making, it doesn't matter how good you are. Soon you'll be packing up and going back to your day job.

However, when your work is being judged by the same people who do what you do, it's another story entirely. The members of the CMA are the performers, organizations, and others involved in "Country Music, directly and substantially," according to literature put out by what has often been called "the world's most active trade organization."

LeAnn Rimes was too smart to expect to be nominated as a major act during her first year. As a person who hopes to, and plans to, have a singing career for a long time to come, she knew she had years to climb that ladder of success. She wants all the years of her stardom to be special ones. She knows that no matter how good people think you are, there's always another level to reach, another accomplishment to aspire to. Besides, most of her heroes in the business had waited through many years and many songs to get the accolades and awards that they proudly display in their homes and management offices.

Vince Gill has won the most CMA Awards—seventeen—in categories ranging from Song to Album to Vocal Event to Male Vocalist to Entertainer of the Year. Garth Brooks has won nine, which puts him up there with some of country's most beloved acts, including Chet Atkins, Alabama, and the Statler Brothers. Numerous other performers have been honored over the years, and even those with only one CMA Award to their credit consider receiving it a magical moment in their careers.

Of course, LeAnn had received many trophies and first-prize ribbons for the talent contests she participated in, so she was no stranger to being singled out as a given evening's most extraordinary performer. But LeAnn hadn't won every contest she entered, so she was prepared for whatever happened with the CMA nominations.

On August 13, 1996, at a press conference on the steps of the Opryhouse, the 1996 CMA nominations were announced. The awards would be presented in a nationally televised ceremony on October 2. Not coincidentally, October Is Country Music Month is a worldwide celebration, and the CMA Awards kick it off.

LeAnn Rimes received two nominations. "Blue" was nominated as Single of the Year and, even more exciting, LeAnn was nominated for the prestigious Horizon Award. The latter was designed to reward the performer who has shown the most progress over the past year. All performers are eligible, but CMA's members and seven thousand eligible voters tend to view it as a newcomer prize.

"Being nominated for two CMA Awards, that's like the biggest highlight of my life, 'cause that's what I've dreamed about since I was a little girl sitting in front of the TV watching Reba get an award."

There went those headlines again! She was the youngest person ever to be nominated in the thirty-year history of the Country Music Awards. Before LeAnn, the youngest was Tanya Tucker, who was nominated at fourteen and won her first award when she was fifteen, back in 1973.

LeAnn told *TV Guide,* "This has been the biggest surprise in my life. I really didn't expect it, because this is my first year in the business. I'm not really expecting an award, but just to be nominated is really neat for me. To think that the people in the business think so highly of me and my music is really an honor. I'll be at the show with bells on."

As if her nominations weren't enough excitement for one day, LeAnn opened for Vince Gill in Nashville that night.

WHO IS TANYA TUCKER?

A true overnight sensation at the age of thirteen with her sexy debut song, "Delta Dawn," in 1972, Tanya Tucker also had the full support of her family when her talent became apparent. From her birthplace in Seminole, Texas, in 1958, Tanya and her family moved first to Phoenix and later to Las Vegas to pursue her career. Boy, did it happen fast. Tanya's first demo tape found its way to the right ears, and she was signed to Columbia Records.

After the smash hit "Delta Dawn" won her attention and praise for her gritty voice and mature delivery—and crossed over to become a big pop hit—Tanya gave her audience several more, including "Would You Lay with Me (In a Field of Stone)."

She was on and off the record charts throughout the late 1970s and 1980s. Supermarket tabloid headlines screeched about this hard-partying young woman and her romance with Glen Campbell. She also went on to become an actress in several made-for-TV and feature films.

In 1991, Tanya Tucker was named CMA Female Vocalist of the Year. In the early 1990s, she had several hits on the country and pop charts, including "It's a Little Too Late." Her *Greatest Hits 1990–92* album, released in April 1993, was certified platinum on February 17, 1995. She continues to be a force in today's music scene and, after two decades in show business, will reach the ripe old age of forty in 1998.

TANYA'S THOUGHTS ON LeANN

ON LeANN'S VOICE
"I think LeAnn has a good voice. It's great to hear a Patsy Cline influence on the radio."

ON EDUCATION
"If I had any advice for her, it would be to stay in school and get her education. It will make her more confident onstage, in communicating with the audience, and in anything else she chooses to do in life."

WHAT TO STUDY
"Stick with at least two subjects in school:
English, which will give her confidence in
talking with the press, and history. She
needs to know where she came from before
she knows where she's going."

ON A NEW TEEN SENSATION
"I'm amazed it's taken this long for someone else to make this kind of debut. But I
think it's well deserved."

ON THE FUTURE
"It's not going to be easy, but I think it's
great she's getting a head start."

LeAnn waved and smiled as her fans at the Kitsap
County Fair in Bremerton, Washington, whistled,
screamed, and clapped for her in the rodeo arena.
Moments later, as she started her set with an a cappella
performance of "Blue Moon of Kentucky," it was so
quiet you could hear the grass grow. Her band joined in
on the third verse and everyone started singing along.

LeAnn looked sharper than sharp in her black boots, tight
black slacks, a black-and-white horizontal-striped blouse,
revealing a little midriff, and a red vinyl jacket.

Teenagers love to wear cool clothes—and LeAnn is no
exception.

"I love to shop," LeAnn admitted. "The guys on the bus are mad at me because I haven't been home and all my clothes are taking up the whole bus!"

It was the same scene at the Wyoming State Fair, at a one-nighter in Anchorage, and another in Vancouver. People showed up bearing flowers for LeAnn and toting cameras in the hope of having their pictures taken with her. Young girls loved her, older fans responded to her vocal echoes of Patsy Cline, and even some guys in cowboy hats lined up, perhaps hoping for a chance to stand close to her for just a moment.

At a bowling party in Nashville a few days before her fourteenth birthday on August 28, LeAnn experienced another first. Everybody started smearing cake all over each other's faces.

"It was really funny," LeAnn said. "We had a great time. But I've never had a food fight before in my life. My forty-year-old friends were starting a food fight, and it was like, 'Oh my goodness.'"

LeAnn later reported she got a "diamond tennis bracelet, and a bunch of money, and anything else you can imagine. This was my best birthday ever."

Two days later, LeAnn headed to the Midwest for four dates. She was the opening act for one of her idols. What did Wynonna have to say to her? "She advised me to keep my head on straight and not let stuff get to me," LeAnn said.

In early September, after playing shows in Columbus and Cincinnati, LeAnn achieved another career high in New York City. The Ed Sullivan Theater on Broadway is where Elvis Presley made his TV debut, where the Beatles enraptured their American fans in 1964, and where circus acts, comedians, and magicians once charmed live audiences and the millions at home every Sunday night. If Ed Sullivan were still alive and broadcasting the show, there's no doubt LeAnn would have performed on it when she was seven or eight.

The theater had lain empty for a long time until CBS restored it for the *Late Show with David Letterman*. Now LeAnn was on its legendary stage singing "Blue."

"You're lucky," Mr. Letterman told her. "You now know what you love to do and what you will do for the rest of your life. A lot of people never figure that out. Me, for example."

LeAnn just beamed her sensational smile. Two days later, she was back on the concert circuit. Seeing LeAnn in live shows proved to devotees and doubters alike that the voice they heard on the record was real, not spiffed up by all the tricks that can be done in the recording studio.

A round piece of wood was carefully taken out of the center of the stage of downtown Nashville's Ryman Auditorium before the Grand Ole Opry moved ten miles away to its new home. That chunk of wood, a small but deeply significant piece of country music's history, was installed in the new Opryhouse at Opryland, built in 1974. Some of country music's all-time legends—including Porter Wagoner, Bill Monroe, Little Jimmy Dickens, Grandpa Jones, and Skeeter Davis—have stood on that sacred spot performing for a live audience. At the same time, they entertained millions of fans as radio station

WSM broadcast what has become the longest-running radio show in the United States.

It is the ultimate dream of every country performer to be a part of the Grand Ole Opry. On September 13, 1996, two weeks after her fourteenth birthday, LeAnn Rimes took her turn at the Opry stage.

"It'll make me proud to see her on it," Wilbur said before the show. "Everybody that's been anybody has been across that stage. It will be a proud night."

Mike Curb himself joined LeAnn onstage to present her with gold and platinum records for *Blue*.

LeAnn said, "It's been a dream of mine for a long time to sing where so many greats have been."

Patsy Cline didn't realize that dream until she was twenty-three.

"How many kids do you know get a gold record for their birthday?" The man asking that question was none other than legendary CBS reporter and news anchor Dan Rather, introducing LeAnn Rimes in a segment for the network's *48 Hours*. As always, Dan Rather asked a good question.

"Well, the young lady you're about to meet, for one," he continued. "Susan Spencer catches up with LeAnn Rimes, spinning gold from a song called 'Blue.'"

Now, imagine being from Pearl, Mississippi, and Garland, Texas, or anywhere in the United States, for that matter. So, sure, you've been to New York City a few times in your life. LeAnn had visited Manhattan as a young child with her godparents and had even dined at Sardi's, the most famous restaurant on Broadway and in the whole theater world.

What could possibly prepare you to have a gold record? And to have a reporter and a camera crew from one of television's most respected and watched news shows following you around the Big Apple as you explore the city, go shopping, and see the sights? Who wouldn't love to be LeAnn Rimes on this bright autumn day in one of the world's greatest cities?

LeAnn introduced Wilbur—"My dad is my producer and comanager"—and Belinda—"My mother just kind of helps out with everything." It must have been equally exciting and probably a little nerve-racking, too, for Wilbur and Belinda to be on national TV.

"I sit in amazement of her," Wilbur told Susan Spencer. "At fourteen, somebody spoke to me, all I could do was look at my feet, you know? She is the pride and joy of my life, Miss LeAnn Rimes, my daughter."

LeAnn told Spencer that the last three months on the road, being introduced as the artist with the number one country album in America, had been, in one word, "crazy."

Turning fourteen in the midst of the biggest success of her life, and hearing herself described for the millionth time as a teenage phenomenon, LeAnn Rimes again made it clear that she had a longer view of her career. "I just hope that down the road," she said, "they're calling me a twenty-one-year-old singing sensation."

As millions of American students reentered their schools in the fall, LeAnn continued her studies with her tutor. Because she had been skipped when she would have entered seventh grade, she was now at the high school sophomore level.

* * *

Returning to Dallas on September 22 for her first performance there since the release of *Blue*, LeAnn Rimes had come home. She performed at a place called Country 2000, a honky-tonk off I-35 that sports enough neon to be a discotheque. Though she had a cold that forced her to cancel a show in St. Louis the night before, LeAnn didn't disappoint her hometown fans.

Before the show, Belinda told a reporter, "I try to make sure she eats right and gets enough rest. That's what mothers are supposed to do. When I go to bed, I pray for everyone on the bus, and I pray for the bus driver."

Marty Rendelman observed, "Belinda is the sweetest human being. All this has to be driving her crazy. She's a little skittish with the media; she's shy."

When she took to the stage, LeAnn was once again the total professional everyone had come to rely on. She was sensational. No one in the audience suspected she had so much as a sniffle.

Singing a great mix of songs from the album, plus such classics as Patsy Cline's "Leavin' on Your Mind," Ben E. King's "Stand by Me," and Hank Williams's "I'm So Lonesome I Could Cry," LeAnn inspired everyone in the audience.

The young girls dancing around the floor perhaps felt they, too, could one day be onstage. The grandparents in the audience looked at LeAnn and thought of their wonderful, talented, beautiful grandchildren.

And even those who were just waiting through the set for the activities that would take place later in the evening couldn't help but look, listen, and stand in awe of the local girl who had made her dream come true.

* * *

The family-owned 350-seat Trail Dust Steak House in Arlington has an upstairs balcony with a great view. Photos of America's favorite actors in classic Western films are flanked by horseshoes, branding irons, mule bits, and other ranch implements. A shiny stainless-steel sliding pond is clearly the quickest route to the dance floor to strut your stuff to live country music seven nights a week

In late September, LeAnn became the major spokesperson for the restaurant. Ads proclaim, "LeAnn Rimes rides with the 'Dust.'" Doug Parker, Trail Dust's cofounder, said, "Everybody in our company is excited and honored to have LeAnn on board with us. She's been a regular customer at our Trail Dust in Dallas for a number of years, knows what we're all about, and believes in what we're doing and what we stand for."

On October 2, 1996, with millions of people around the world watching, the 1996 Country Music Association Awards show was broadcast from the Grand Ole Opry stage in Nashville, Tennessee.

Wilbur Rimes claimed he was more nervous before the show than LeAnn was. Apparently, that was nothing new. Always caught up in the whirlwind surrounding her, LeAnn nevertheless manages to be the calm within the storm. "The bigger the pressure, the better she does," Wilbur said. Again, what comes from within LeAnn Rimes is the full confidence that she can meet any challenge and the knowledge that her voice is a force all its own that will never let her down.

Forth Worth's KTVT channel 11 broadcast a preview

show. One of the station's staff members interviewed LeAnn in the balcony of the Arlington Music Hall and talked about her years as part of Johnnie High's Country Music Revue. A director's chair with her name on the back has a special place in the women's dressing room, celebrating another chapter in the building's history. Photos of LeAnn and articles about her are scattered throughout the old theater.

Johnnie High was also on the TV show. "This is my world," he said. "I enjoy this more than I would out in the big world. It's more intimate here."

Live from Opryland on the stage of the Grand Ole Opry, the 1996 CMA Awards show opened with LeAnn Rimes singing "Blue." Countless millions of current and future fans in the United States, Canada, and a dozen foreign nations watched the bright new star on TV. And watching from the audience were people who'd helped make her a star: Wilbur and Belinda, who had to be feeling as if they were in a dream of their own; Bill Mack, for whom LeAnn had fulfilled the long-held dream of not only making "Blue" a hit but singing it the way this veteran had heard it in his heart when he first wrote it; and, in the fourth row, courtesy of friends who'd given them tickets, sat Johnnie High with his wife, Wanda.

LeAnn had a beautiful red gown made for the CMA Awards. But then she decided she wanted to wear something in—guess what?—blue. The full-length gown with a velvet top and taffeta skirt she finally selected was perfect. With every shining blond hair in place, she looked grown up and classic and gorgeous.

Poised and proud, she lifted the microphone to her lips and sang as if she'd been practicing her whole life for this moment. In fact, she had been.

The members of the Country Music Association gave her a long standing ovation. Beloved country singer Vince Gill, hosting the show, teased her a little, like an older brother, after inviting her back up on the stage to take another bow. Nashville was showing LeAnn its warmest welcome to date. The new star from Mississippi and Texas was now an official member, or at least an honorary citizen, of Music City.

Later in the show, LeAnn sang Patsy Montana's signature song, "I Want to Be a Cowboy's Sweetheart." Montana, who spent most of her eighty-two years on the road entertaining audiences of all ages, had died in May 1996. Now LeAnn was given the honor of helping the CMA pay tribute to her dear friend and mentor. LeAnn also helped the CMA induct Montana into the Country Music Hall of Fame.

LeAnn didn't win either award for which she was nominated. The Horizon Award went to Bryan White. (LeAnn has an autographed picture of him in her bus.) George Strait, from Poteet, Texas, by the way, won for Single of the Year with "Check Yes or No." Strait is considered to be one of the most important reasons for the surge in country music's popularity in the 1980s. Garth Brooks has credited him with helping pave the way for his own phenomenal success in the late eighties and early nineties.

Was she disappointed not to win? "No," she said, "because it was my first year in the business. I didn't even vote for myself at first. It's important to me to win [eventually], because it's something that I've dreamed of for a long time, but this year it was just too soon."

What she did attain was the all-important respect and affection of the kings and queens of country music, assembled in the Grand Ole Opry for all the world to see. And Johnnie High stated flatly to a newspaper reporter that LeAnn is "the biggest thing that has ever happened to country music. More important than Elvis."

Oh, and another thing. The week after the Country Music Awards presentation, sales of the album doubled.

"I've been in the business thirty years, and I have never seen anything like this," said Dennis Hannon, executive vice-president and general manager of Curb Records. "It's a marketing man's dream."

The album stayed on the charts at number one until new releases by longtime country stars Alan Jackson and Reba McEntire came along later in the year and pushed LeAnn to number three. Soon it was back up to number one.

Two days after the CMAs, on October 4, LeAnn played for ten thousand people in Harbor Park in Norfolk, Virginia.

"This is the largest headline crowd I've ever played to," she said. Nervous? "No, I don't get nervous anymore. I concentrate on the show." Before and after the show, LeAnn met the press. When they asked her about going out on dates, Wilbur commented, "She's been asked those same questions thousands of times."

In October, LeAnn said, "We really haven't been home for two days since July twenty-eighth. It's pretty busy. I'm holding up fine. I'm having a good time."

* * *

On November 4, 1996, LeAnn appeared at the Cowboy Boogie Company in Anaheim, California. Two days later, she played at the Ventura Theater in Ventura.

The pop-music critic for the *Los Angeles Times*, Robert Hilburn, wrote, "For most of her set, Rimes had the audience virtually spellbound. . . . It takes a solid performer to keep the customers satisfied at the massive club . . . you could hear the gasps of surprise and delight when Rimes took to the stage and began applying that character-soaked voice to tales of sexual yearning and lingering heartbreak."

On December 18, LeAnn sang "One Way Ticket (Because I Can)" on *The Tonight Show with Jay Leno.* Jay couldn't stop smiling at her.

On December 23, LeAnn was part of a morning Christmas party at KPLX radio station. A few lucky fans were invited in, and LeAnn signed autographs between her on-air interviews. Dallas mayor Ron Kirk and police chief Ben Click stopped in.

"Forget Troy, I'm here to see LeAnn," Kirk said. Troy Aikman has a show on Mondays called *Aikman at 8.*

"I'm happy to see all the success you've been having," Aikman told LeAnn.

December 27, 1996. More than six thousand incredibly excited fans in the standing-room-only audience were waiting to hear LeAnn close out the most fabulous year of her life. Very few artists have ever sold out Billy Bob's on the strength of only their second record.

"This girl is on fire and deservedly so," said "Billy Bob's Texas Round-Up," a monthly newsletter. "She has a great show, and her stage presence is that of a seasoned veteran."

The proudest man in the audience was Thad Butler, LeAnn's granddaddy. "They were turning people away," he said during a talk in his home in Pearl, Mississippi, about a month later. "It's the first time she played there since she became a star."

"LeAnn's amazing. We could have easily sold another two thousand tickets," said Pam Minick, Billy Bob's marketing director. "We turned away a lot of folks."

Now, with her hot single—"One Way Ticket (Because I Can)"—sitting pretty in the top ten, LeAnn was having a ball on the stage at Billy Bob's.

Someone in the audience yelled, "We love you." LeAnn's smile turned into a huge grin and she shouted, "I love you, too!"

CHAPTER SEVEN
☆ ☆ ☆
Because I Can

The Dixie National Rodeo in Jackson, Mississippi, was in full swing.

More than 2,500 horses, 350 wagons, 300 floats, a procession of antique cars, and 5 bands and dance groups marched out of gate number one at the Mississippi State Fairgrounds on a Saturday morning this past February. They strutted through the streets of downtown Jackson in the Dixie National Parade. At dozens of events over the course of ten days, everyone feasted on great food, whistled and cheered at rodeos, and witnessed Civil War reenactments.

The girls and boys of the show choirs—the Impressions and Sugar and Spice—had just finished their performances at the sold-out show in the Mississippi Coliseum. They were the opening acts for that night's concert headliner.

Their teacher, Amy Arender Hogue, showered the young singers with praise and love. Now the students of Mississippi Arts in Motion in Brandon were to be quiet and wait patiently. Soon another of Amy's talented students from Rankin County would take her turn on the stage.

All the excitement of the largest rodeo east of the Mississippi River was now focused on their hometown wonder, Miss LeAnn Rimes.

And the crowd went wild! The Texas fans at Billy Bob's had been rooting for LeAnn since she was six or seven. Well, Mississippi had one up on the Lone Star State. LeAnn had been their baby, their niece, their cousin, their neighbor, their schoolmate. She'd graced every stage in Rankin County before she was six. Texas might claim her now, but Mississippi really knew her when.

All day and night, people had been calling Thad Butler for tickets to the show but he couldn't help. "They done waited too late," he said.

The sweetheart of the rodeo sang "Blue," and there wasn't a dry eye in the house. She and her Blue Country band slammed through "Cowboy's Sweetheart," broke hearts with "I Will Always Love You," and nearly exploded the place with "One Way Ticket (Because I Can)."

Thad Butler wasn't the least surprised when the audience gave LeAnn a long standing ovation. "Look," he said, "LeAnn rocks the building when she comes on. They go crazy over LeAnn everywhere she goes."

When she was finally allowed to stop playing encores and leave the stage, LeAnn went backstage and reveled in the hugs, kisses, and love of the many friends and family members who'd come to see her. Then she invited the seventeen students from the show choirs and their parents backstage. Although she was quite tired, according to Hogue, LeAnn took time with each child.

"The kids were very excited," Amy said. "One little girl took out five one-dollar bills and made her autograph each one. LeAnn just did it for her. All the kids were wearing bandannas and she signed all their bandannas, too."

LeAnn loves doing nice things for kids. When she played Sam's Town Casino near Memphis, she met a group of children for an autograph session in a nearby hotel where minors were allowed.

Another night she did for twelve-year-old singer Kalli Roan what Patsy Montana had once done for her. "Thirty minutes before I went onstage," said Kalli about her evening at Johnnie High's in Arlington, "LeAnn and her dad walked through the front door on a surprise visit. I was really nervous when I sang, because LeAnn was watching.

"Afterward, I was walking back to the dressing room when I felt a hand on my shoulder. It was LeAnn's. She told me I did good, and that meant so much to me. I will never forget it."

If any of her young fans have a fraction of the success that LeAnn had in 1996, they'll be doing just fine, thank you.

In *Billboard's* special year-end double issue, Chet Flippo wrote, "LeAnn Rimes came roaring out of Texas with a fresh approach to an old song, taking 'Blue' to instant superstardom."

LeAnn was named a Chart Topper. *Blue* was one of only seven albums that went to number one on the Top Country Albums chart between January 6 and December 28, 1996. It had spent an amazing nineteen weeks in the number one position, more than any other album that year.

LeAnn's phenomenal success was not limited to America. In country-music-friendly Australia, the album went triple platinum. It also went double platinum in Canada, and gold in England.

LeAnn was the number one Country Singles Sales Artist of the year with "Blue."

Rolling Stone asked various artists to pick their top-ten favorite albums of the year. LeAnn might have been puzzled but Wilbur probably laughed out loud when he heard that Gene Simmons, of the notorious heavy-makeup rock group Kiss, named *Blue* his favorite album of the year. It was the only country album on a list that included Van Halen, Nine Inch Nails, and Garbage.

Country Music Television ranked "Blue" the number four video of the year, based on chart position, time on the chart, song- and video-production quality, viewer requests, and entertainment value. They also named LeAnn the Female Rising Video Star of the Year.

The director of the "Blue" video, Chris Rogers, won two *Billboard* Video Music Awards: Best Country Music Video of the Year and Best New Artist Video of the Year. This recognition led to the video being played on VH-1 and MTV.

Although the country-music business closed out 1996 with a twelve-percent drop in sales, LeAnn Rimes was selling records faster than her company could press them.

* * *

Country America magazine's February 1997 cover headline roared out beneath a great photo of LeAnn. LEADER OF THE PACK. LEANN RIMES HEADS THE COUNTRY AMERICA TOP TEN NEW STARS.

New Country put LeAnn on the cover with Johnny Cash in its Year's Best issue. "LeAnn Rimes is the new generation. At the age of fourteen," the magazine said, "she has already sold two million albums, singing songs that span generations, with a style that transcends generations. Together, the Man in Black and the young woman in 'Blue' demonstrate country's reach."

As of January, LeAnn was booked for thirty-two dates with Alan Jackson in 1997, including one in Reunion Arena, where she used to sing the National Anthem.

LeAnn's Christmas hadn't been half bad either.

She visited the White House to help light the White House Christmas tree and met Bill and Hillary Clinton. President Clinton complimented the girl from the state next door to his own.

"The president was real nice," LeAnn said. "He told me that he had my CD and he enjoyed my music—he's a big fan of mine."

The Rimeses spend the holidays—almost two whole weeks—at home in Texas. They got a new Peterbus— that's a tour bus to us civilians—with a blue-and-white interior, more closet space, a study area, and a tanning booth. Now LeAnn, Wilbur, and Belinda would travel separately from the band. After living in a Garland apartment for eight years, they bought a large house with a pool in Dallas. The first item in the living room was the drum set Wilbur bought LeAnn for Christmas.

Over the holidays, the family could watch TV ads, sponsored by the Target chain, of LeAnn dancing with Bugs Bunny and other cartoon characters. She sang a great little toe-tapper, "Put a Little Holiday in Your Heart," which was the A-side of a promotional CD that shoppers got if they bought *Blue*. The flip side featured the cut of "Unchained Melody" that had been recorded but not included on the album.

Also on TVs from coast to coast was Oprah Winfrey's show on "People Who Made It in 1996." Gee, guess LeAnn qualified for that!

Introducing LeAnn as "the teenager who soared to the top of the *Billboard* charts in 1996," Oprah said, "It was a very good year for her and she's only fourteen years old."

LeAnn came out and sang "Blue" to a standing ovation.

Oprah told LeAnn that her own attempts at singing make her dogs howl. Two of America's favorite ladies discussed LeAnn's journey to the top and her education through home schooling. Then Oprah invited her to teach the audience how to yodel, an exercise that proved you either have the yodeling muscle in your throat or you don't!

Didn't LeAnn miss school and the prom and all that? LeAnn had been asked that question all year long.

"I don't think I'm really giving up a lot, because I'm achieving a lot right now," she said. "I do have a different life, and I've grown up in an adult world. I don't have any friends my age. I don't mind that. I don't mind giving up the prom kind of thing and all that. I really don't think I'm missing out on anything 'cause this is what I want to do."

If you get gold and platinum records for your birthday, what's left to get for Christmas? How about your very first number one radio hit single!

Released to radio on October 9, "One Way Ticket (Because I Can)" jumped out of the speakers and shot up the charts to number one with (no pun intended) record speed. Wade Jesson, *Billboard*'s "Country Corner" columnist, said, "LeAnn's first radio chart-topping song turns the conservative tide at country radio."

Remember when "Blue" was too traditional for some stations? Well, some traditional stations thought at first that "One Way Ticket" may have gone too far in the other direction—because of its distinctively pop sound

However, country fans once again made their opinions known through enthusiastic phone calls to the stations, which resulted in putting the song in heavy rotation on playlists. Sales of *Blue* also rose.

In *Billboard*'s October 12 review of "One Way Ticket," Larry Flick said, "Rimes's latest outing is a vibrant, uptempo number. The song is strong, and the production has a lot of energy, but it is Rimes's performance that elevates the song from other female, uptempo, country radio fare. The impressive set of pipes she displays on her ballads also serves her well on this tune."

"One Way Ticket (Because I Can)" is the third number one hit single cowritten by respected Nashville songwriter Keith Hinton. "A Little Less Talk and a Lot More Action," written with Jimmy Stewart for singer Toby Keith, and "Heart of a Woman" for Billy Ray Cyrus with Bret Cartwright, also rose to the top on radio.

Hinton was asked to explain to people outside the music business the process behind writing a song.

"I take a title and I write from that," Hinton said. "I immediately figured out where 'because I can' should come in the song, but the whole thing starts with the 'I'm gonna,' well, gonna do what?

"It's that the sky's the limit, basically I can, I can do all these things, that was the concept, it was basically a laundry list of things that I can do . . . and why? Because I can. It's that simple, and usually it's your simple thoughts that make hit songs."

Why does he think it appealed to LeAnn?

"I think the basic thing that she really liked was stepping out there and saying 'because I can,' and it went right down the pocket of what her career goals were, her desire to take this talent out and show the world that she can do this.

"Because she's fourteen, she has that 'I can conquer the world' thing that young people have that generally gets beat out of us as we grow older, and she still has it. You can call it naïveté or just that wonderful ability to believe that all things are possible."

Hinton played guitar with Billy Ray on two albums, and on Cyrus's mega–number one, "Achy Breaky Heart." Hinton has also worked with female singers and writers "who need a producer's hand, guitar-player foil, and somebody to cowrite with."

With that background and experience, why does Hinton think LeAnn does such a good job with "One Way Ticket"?

"That is something that you can't put your finger on, but it's all through that vocal. Obviously you can't sing that song if you don't believe that, and she did. This was definitely the case of giving her the ball and she ran with it hard and scored a big touchdown."

LeAnn's first number one radio single was her "one way ticket" into the new year. The week of January 8, 1997, "One Way Ticket" was the number one video on CMT.

"The biggest part of what I like about doing videos is to see your music actually come to life," LeAnn says. "You get to see it put on film, to see the story line, and it shows what the song is all about. The first time I saw myself, I was kind of shocked. It was like—I did that video."

"I loved the video," Hinton said. "I was tickled to death that the colors were so bright and it was so young. I liked the fact that it was one of the few videos that goes along with what the song says—the fact that she's in San Francisco, which is as far west as you can go, and she's on the roof of the streetcar, which is the one way ticket on the train. The sun's shining, the wind's blowing, her hair's in her face."

The clothes are great, too, from a mint green suit with a little fur collar to shiny blue form-fitting pants. Walking around San Francisco's beautiful streets, carrying shopping bags, and stopping to flirt, LeAnn is a girl on top of the world as well as a woman emerging to take her place in that world.

About "One Way Ticket" one radio programmer said, "The novelty has worn off the age thing, but she's just an incredible talent."

When the Grammy nominations were announced on January 8, LeAnn Rimes was the only country act nominated for New Artist of the Year. The New Artist award, established in 1967, has been won by vocal giants Carly Simon, Bette Midler, Natalie Cole, and Mariah Carey. LeAnn was also nominated for Female Country Vocal Performance. "Blue" by Bill Mack was nominated not only as Country Song of the Year but in the overall category of Song of the Year.

"I'm loving this," LeAnn said. "It's a lot of fun. I really don't know if I should enjoy it too much, because it'll get to me. Sometimes people enjoy it way too much and get the big head."

The American Music Awards (the AMAs), produced by Dick Clark, cover all categories of music. The awards are voted on by a national sampling of approximately twenty thousand people, taking into account age, sex, geographic location, and ethnic origin. LeAnn was nominated for Favorite New Country Artist.

The Rimeses had just returned from Australia's version of Fan Fair, where fans had made LeAnn the best-selling female artist of all time in their country. They cheered like mad at a music festival in Tamworth when she sang "Blue."

Back in the USA, LeAnn enjoyed the rehearsals for the AMA with her fellow nominees Terri Clark and Mindy McCready. On January 27, the show was broadcast live on ABC from the Shrine Auditorium in Los Angeles.

Looking magnificent in red (the dress she'd had made in Nashville for the CMAs before deciding to wear the blue one), LeAnn sang "Unchained Melody."

Then she won.

"It feels wonderful. This is my first award," LeAnn said after accepting the award for Favorite New Country Artist.

"Everything that has happened to me in the last six months usually happens to an artist in two or three years. Getting this award to go along with everything else is overwhelming."

Backstage, Dick Clark told her that everywhere he goes people in all categories of music want to hear about LeAnn. "The people we call mature rock-and-rollers are converting to country by the thousands, continuously, because they understand the music," he said.

Three weeks after the AMAs, a supermarket tabloid published an article and picture of LeAnn at the awards show: WHOEVER TARTED UP FOURTEEN-YEAR-OLD LEANN RIMES—BEST NEW COUNTRY ARTIST—TO LOOK LIKE A HONKY-TONK HARLOT SHOULD BE STRUNG UP.

Of all the nerve! That tabloid should be strung up! Don't listen to them, Belinda—you've always done a superb job. And LeAnn, you've always looked just right.

* * *

"My image is me. What I love, the music that I love, the clothes I enjoy wearing. Just being me is my image and no one has ever tried to change that.

"I just pick clothes that I like. I wear stuff everyone else my age and older would wear, because I've grown up in an adult world and I have to handle myself in a mature way. I guess I've grown up fast, but I really don't mind at all."

The "age thing," as LeAnn calls it, came up frequently in interviews all summer long, and it was clear that it bothered her a little. Although it has been a way to get her noticed, it's something she'd like people to forget as they listen to her music.

"I never wanted to be known as a fourteen-year-old singing sensation. I just want to be known as an artist," she said. "Hopefully, people don't have to think of me as fourteen to say, 'She's good.' Hopefully, they can say, 'She's good because she's good.'"

That may not happen as easily as she hopes. The thirteen-year-old sensation will one day be the seventeen-year-old sensation, and even in her twenties she will be remembered, like Tanya Tucker and Brenda Lee, as "that girl who started so young."

One reviewer thought LeAnn's youth was a problem in relation to some of the songs on *Blue*. She never misses a note or a mood or even makes the songs sound suggestive in any way. Still, "My Baby," a sexy tribute to the way a man makes a woman feel, and "Good Lookin' Man," celebrating the male physique, raise the question that maybe she's "too young to be flirting with sexual innuendo."

"Yeah, some of the lyrics do bother me," Belinda agreed.

LeAnn doesn't date and "won't for a long time if I can help it," said Wilbur.

What does Mom think?

"She's a mom." LeAnn sighed. "She's the worrier in the family."

What about boyfriends? "I don't have time for anybody now. Seriously, I don't," LeAnn said. "Maybe one of these days when things slow down a little."

"Like when you get to be about twenty-five," Wilbur added.

What about falling in love? Will the young artist who sang "I Will Always Love You" with such heartbreaking emotion ever have the time for a real relationship?

"I know that it's gonna be hard for anyone in this business," she said. "What I'm kind of worried about is that people would think of me as 'LeAnn Rimes' and not as me, you know what I mean? You don't know what people want you for anymore. It's scary. I know it's like that for any kind of successful person. But we'll see how that goes."

LeAnn's already done quite a few charity events. Country-music stars are enormously generous with their time and talent. That translates into huge amounts of money for the many deserving charities whose fund-raising galas they attend—and to whom they often contribute quietly.

"I love children and old people, and I am anxious to use my new celebrity to help charities that provide assistance to these two groups," she said.

"The best thing is meeting fans," LeAnn said. "They seem to love my songs, and that inspires me to make the

best music and put on the best show I can. It just blows
me away that people are liking my music this much. It
really does.

"I could not ask for better fans. They've been great to
me. They're absolutely wonderful."

LeAnn has said time and again that she wants her
generation to "know where the roots of country are."
She's been making that happen since she was a little girl.

"What I'm hearing from fans now is that they're wanting this traditional country. The kids that are twenty and
under, who might not have heard Hank Williams, Sr.,
and Patsy Cline, now they're knowing this music
because I'm singing it. When they come to the concert,
they love it, because it is so different."

Everything old is new again. The big talk around
Music Row these days is about a return to traditional
country. LeAnn can take her share of the credit for that
phenomenon.

Veteran music-business pros have nothing but respect
for her—and not as a kid or a novelty or some kind of
"teen sensation." They know better than anyone that it
will take more than that to sustain a career.

"She's a great singer; there's absolutely no doubt
about the fact that she has a great instrument," says
Keith Hinton. "There are certain people who I would
say are born singers. Some people who can sing are
very good at it, but I don't consider them to be born
singers. Born singers are like Barbra Streisand, and
LeAnn is definitely one of those. She's known what she
wanted to do since she was five, and it's obvious that
she made the right choice. This is not something that

she comes by lightly or that somebody talked her into. This is something that is so innate and it comes out of her and it's unstoppable. For that reason I think she's going to have a big future."

LeAnn told 48 Hours, "There are very few people that stay around in the business for a long time. Hopefully, people are liking my voice and my music more than they are thinking about my age . . . I think that's the way I'm going to be able to stay around."

As a big star with a tremendous sales record, LeAnn and her producers will have their pick of the best songs being written inside or outside Nashville.

"I want to have the freedom to do the songs I like. If I sing little-kid songs about getting out of high school and stuff like that, I'm not gonna make it. I'm trying to appeal to everybody from four to eighty.

"Country music is not just Texas—it's the whole United States, the whole world. I think there's a lot of great artists who have come out of Texas, but I'm going for broader appeal. . . . What I wanna keep doing . . . is traditional and contemporary country . . . a wide spectrum of music for everybody and for all age-groups."

Like Patsy Cline and Celine Dion—and probably many others whose talent is such a force—LeAnn was so sure of her future that she wasn't surprised when it happened. "I don't know how I knew, but I just knew.

"Shania and a lot of other women in music have definitely paved the way for people like me to come along. The new women in country music and the new women in other types of music have caused newcomers like me to step up to where they've been."

Five out of the top-ten country artists today are female—and one of them is LeAnn Rimes. Of course.

"I never doubted LeAnn for one minute," Johnnie High said. "This is a crazy business—a lot of people out there, sometimes they deserve success and they don't get it. But I was raised on a farm, and we would milk the cows at night, and when you woke up in the morning, the cream was at the top. It's kind of that way in this case—the ones that are really great somehow, some way, it seems to happen to them.

"I hope I've had a good influence," High said. "Not only me, but the band here, the regulars, and the fans, so she will be stable and mature and not get off into things she shouldn't be doing."

Does Beverly Smith think all this success will go to LeAnn's head? "I hope not," she said. "Her parents are good Christian people, and they seem to have a handle on it."

"With a fourteen-year-old, you have to be there. You have to make it as normal as possible," Belinda said. "She is a teenager and she is mature, both in body and spirit. Sometimes she thinks she's older than she is, and that scares me, but she is a wonderful kid."

Wilbur Rimes is often asked whether in helping his daughter's dream come true he hasn't also risked hurting her by exposing her to the dangers inherent in the entertainment business.

"People come up to me and say, 'What if she turns out like so-and-so? What if she gets on dope?' Well, the prisons are full of people who've been on dope and

never been in the entertainment business. You just have
to make the best of it. If you want to be in the entertainment business and be a good person, you can."

"Her parents saw this coming a long time ago,"
Johnnie High said. "They're prepared."

"We want her to grow up and be a stable human being,
and I hope we can take her through this and make it happen," Wilbur said. "Life's a struggle any way you go at
it. You just hope."

LeAnn is aware of the pitfalls of her sudden success.
"My parents have always looked out for me, to be there
to tell me what's right and wrong. But this is something
I've wanted all my life. I'm very happy."

LeAnn is clear about what she's attained.

"I'm not an overnight success. I've been at this since
I was six. Ten years from now, hopefully, I'll still be
doing what I'm doing. Maybe win a few awards and do
a bit of acting in between here and there.

"This year was a little overwhelming. I didn't know
what to expect. . . . It's been a dream come true."

Back in Texas, Mrs. Nix and the current crop of students at Club Hill Elementary are excited over LeAnn's
success. "The kids have her textbooks with her name in
them," Mrs. Nix said. "Some of them write to her. She's
come back to the school and we're trying to get her to
come again. She has stayed as sweet and humble as she
was."

Her parents would like LeAnn's career to remain a
mom-and-pop operation. They're no strangers to the
business: After all, they've been at it for more than a
decade. Besides, how could things get any crazier than

they were in 1996? What more could possibly happen that they haven't learned to cope with already?

Fans who heard LeAnn's version of "Unchained Melody," the flip side of the Target Stores' promotional record, called radio stations asking to hear it. Some stations played the promo copy, and the song soon cracked the top ten of the *Billboard* country charts. In the short but astounding history of LeAnn Rimes, fans created *another* hit with no record in the stores to buy.

On February 11, a CD called *The Early Years* went on sale. Many of the songs were the ones LeAnn had recorded for *All That*. Other songs were added, including "Unchained Melody."

The album debuted at number one on the pop charts as well as number one on the country charts, knocking *Blue* to number two.

The last act to have their second album knock their first one down a slot was the Beatles.

The Early Years also debuted at number one on the *Billboard* 200. This makes LeAnn the first country artist to enter the chart at the top since Garth Brooks. She's only the second country female in history to do it: The first was her sister Mississippian Bobbie Gentry, in October 1967.

So much for taking a minute to rest.

"Music's biggest night" is one way the Grammy Awards are described every year. This year, the night was even bigger. Broadcasting live from a packed Madison Square Garden, the first time the awards ceremony had been held in such a large house, the show was as dazzling and exciting as New York City itself.

Steve Winwood, Sheryl Crow, and Jakob Dylan came out to present the Grammy for Best New Artist. As the camera swept over the crowd, it stopped for a moment. Millions and millions of people around the world who were tuned in to watch the music business celebrate itself got a glimpse of the only country star to be nominated in that category.

LeAnn Rimes sat in the audience with her parents. She was dressed in a simple sheath of palest blue. A whisper of a necklace and blond waves trickling to her shoulders framed the face everyone had come to love. LeAnn's dad looked sharp in his tuxedo, and her mom looked gorgeous in a pale blue suit. Wilbur C. and Belinda Butler Rimes of Pearl, Mississippi, and Garland, Texas, were beaming.

Earlier that afternoon, LeAnn had won the Grammy for Best Female Country Vocal Performance. Also at the prebroadcast ceremony, when the Grammy for Country Song of the Year was awarded, it went to the man who had waited more than thirty years to hear what he'd had in mind when he'd first written the song.

Bill Mack had won the Country Song of the Year award for "Blue."

He sure had started something for LeAnn when he gave her that song. Songwriters are where the music begins. As Gloria Estefan said later in the broadcast, "If it ain't on the page, it ain't on the stage."

Now, in New York, Bill Mack, radio's longtime Midnight Cowboy, also had a dream come true.

Sheryl Crow read the list of nominations, in alphabetical order, for the Best New Artist Grammy. As each name was read, a snippet of one of their songs was played. Garbage. Jewel. No Doubt. The Tony Rich Project. LeAnn Rimes.

The notes of "Blue" lingered in the air. Steve Winwood, whose own legendary rock-and-roll career had begun when he was a teenager, opened the envelope.

"And the Best New Artist is . . .

"LeAnn Rimes!"

The audience exploded in cheers and applause. And LeAnn Rimes began to cry. She kissed Belinda. She hugged and kissed her producer and manager, Wilbur Rimes, her daddy.

She walked to the stage of Madison Square Garden to accept the first Best New Artist award given to an artist marketed out of Nashville, the first Best New Artist award given to a pure country performer.

"Oh my gosh, I never expected this at all," LeAnn said. "This means more to me than anything in the world.

"First of all, I want to thank my mom and dad and Lyle Walker for everything they've done for me." Her voice broke a little as she continued. "I want to thank all the fans and all of radio for playing my records. Thanks to Rogers and Cowan, and Sandy Friedman, Rod Essig and CAA, and Mike Curb and Curb Records for giving me the opportunity of a lifetime and the freedom to do what I love."

There she stood, looking proud and happy and beautiful for all the world to see.

"I want to thank all my friends back home and all the guys that make it possible on the road.

"I love you very much."

According to the National Academy of Recording

Arts and Sciences, LeAnn Rimes is possibly the youngest person ever to win a Grammy.

By the way, the winner of the first Best New Artist Grammy back in 1967 was Bobbie Gentry.

What dreams are left for LeAnn?

She'd like to have her own house when she gets a little older, "a place on a hill with horses and cows—just a place where I can get away and not be around anybody."

After one of the most universally acclaimed national debuts in entertainment history, her strategy is still "to make the best music I can and do the best concerts I can."

She wants to continue singing and writing songs.

"I want to stay country for as long as I can, but I also want to break out into other things. I've been listening to Barbra Streisand and Celine Dion. I would like to get into the pop field a little bit. I might even try some acting. I want to stay around in this business for a long time.

"I didn't really set a time line for myself. I really just wanted to accomplish my dream of being something."

Real dreamers never stop finding new ways to reach for the stars. And they never stop believing they will achieve everything they want. So—what's LeAnn going to do next?

"Fred's teaching me to play the drums. I always wanted to play the drums. They're neat."

LeANN: WINNER OF FIVE ACADEMY OF
COUNTRY MUSIC NOMINATIONS

The thirty-second annual ACM nominations were announced on March 3, 1997, in California, and guess who made several lists? LeAnn was nominated for the Academy of Country Music New Female Vocalist, along with Deana Carter and Mindy McCready. These women made more than great music in 1996. They also made history.

For the first time, each New Female Vocalist nominee had sold at least one million albums.

The top New Female Vocalist wasn't a huge surprise to LeAnn's fans. The big honor for LeAnn is her nomination for Top Female Vocalist, which puts her in the company of Patty Loveless, Shania Twain, Trisha Yearwood, and Reba McEntire.

Blue was nominated as Album of the Year. And there's even more good news for Bill Mack—Song of the Year and Single of the Year nominations include . . . "Blue."

Jo Sgammato is a writer and journalist who writes about popular culture. A former book-publishing executive, she is also the coauthor of Marjorie Jaffe's *The Muscle Memory Method.* She divides her time between New York and Nashville, where her husband is a producer, manager, and songwriter.

*Lorrie Morgan was born to be
a country-western music star.*

In FOREVER YOURS, FAITHFULLY,
Lorrie Morgan tells her tempestuous story
of sweet triumph and bitter tragedy.
From her childhood as a Nashville blue-
blood, performing at the Grand Ole Opry
at the tender age of eleven, to her turbu-
lent, star-crossed love affair with Keith
Whitley, a bluegrass legend she loved
passionately but could not save from his
personal demons, to her rise to superstardom, she lays bare all the secrets and
great passions of a life lived to the fullest.

And her story would not be complete
without the music that has been her
lifeline.

FOREVER YOURS, FAITHFULLY
by Lorrie Morgan

Published by Ballantine Books.
Available wherever books are sold.

Two is better than one!

COUNTRY'S GREATEST DUO
The Brooks & Dunn Story

by

Jo Sgammato

Just mention foot-stomping honky tonk tunes, rich ballads, stylish videos, and an awesome stage show and people *know* you're talking about Brooks & Dunn. Here is the exciting story of a couple of guys at the top of their form: family men who love to make music, race cars, and thrill fans of all ages and musical tastes.

COUNTRY'S GREATEST DUO
The Brooks & Dunn Story
by Jo Sgammato

Published by Ballantine Books.
Available in bookstores everywhere.

*NASCAR's hottest star
comes roaring to life in . . .*

NATURAL BORN WINNER
The Jeff Gordon Story

by George Mair

Who says you can't have it all? Racing star Jeff Gordon is twenty-six years old, married to a former beauty queen, worshiped by his fans, respected by his rivals, and the youngest Winston Cup Rookie of the Year and Winston Cup champion. Gordon always knew he wanted to drive fast—and he meets that challenge every time he hits the tarmac with the help of the Rainbow Warriors.

A must for every racing fan, NATURAL BORN WINNER tracks Jeff Gordon from his childhood in California and Indiana right up to the 1997 NASCAR season, providing valuable insight into this phenomenal young champion.

Published by Ballantine Books.
Available wherever books are sold.

Printed in the United States
by Baker & Taylor Publisher Services